W

Jo Phillips and David Seymour

First published in Great Britain in 2010 by
Biteback Publishing Ltd
Heal House
375 Kennington Lane
London
SE11 5QY

ISBN 978-1-84954-022-3

10 9 8 7 6 5 4 3 2 1

A CIP catalogue record for this book is available from the British Library.

Set in Garamond
Printed and bound in Great Britain by CPI Cox & Wyman, Reading, RG1 8EX.

Contents

Preface

There is a contradiction at the heart of this book. It is about politics but aimed at people who aren't interested in politics. It wants to persuade you to vote but gives dozens of very good reasons why you shouldn't.

On the positive side, it should give you a few laughs and provide enough trivial information to amaze your friends, astound your boss and make you a champion in pub quizzes.

It's not the sort of self-help book which will get you to lose weight, make you popular, secure a brilliant job or score with loads of stunningly beautiful partners.

But what we hope it might do is persuade you to influence how this country is run.

Read it in any order you like. Take whatever message from it you like. But, as they don't say in all the best blurbs, this book won't change your life – but it could help you to change the world.

The X Factor or the x factor?

The most significant voting trend of the past half-century isn't towards the Left or the Right. Or between military intervention and pacifism. Or choosing to be an active partner in Europe rather than a poodle of the USA or vice versa. Or for or against any set of policies, particular policy or politicians.

This movement involved more than eighteen million people – around 40 per cent of British adults – at the last general election yet it didn't get a single member of Parliament elected. For this is the Apathy Party, the people who can't be bothered or simply refuse to drop into a polling station once every four-or-so years to mark their X on a ballot form.

The number of Britons who vote has plunged from more than four in five in the post-war elections to three in five in the first two of the twenty-first century. At the 2005 election almost twice as many people didn't vote as voted Labour, which still won with a big majority.

Yet we worship the concept of democracy – which is, after all, simply the business of voting representatives in and out – as the iconic symbol of civilised society. Not only do the leaders of the Western world lecture the rest of the planet on its advantages, they will from time to time send in the troops to enforce it on countries suffering under the yoke of dictatorship.

So something is going seriously wrong in Britain if a growing number of citizens feel voting isn't worth bothering with. Why? Let us count the ways.

Some who don't vote are contemptuous of politicians,

especially after the scandal of MPs' expenses and allowances. Why should I bother to lend my support to self-serving prigs, they argue? Others believe 'They' are all the same, 'they' being politicians. The party label makes no difference. Whatever it says on the bottle, the contents come out identical. The government can change but nothing else does.

At least those reasons for not voting are reasons. The same can't be said of people who are simply too lazy or dumb to get off their arses and wander down to the polling station. Others can't be bothered because they know nothing about politics, something they perversely glory in, because they can't see that it has anything to do with them. They consider that politicians inhabit some twilight world to which voters are only let in long enough for them to do their duty at election times before the shutters are slammed shut again.

Politicians are baffled by the severe decline in interest in politics, rather like a passionate football fan not understanding how anyone doesn't share their enthusiasm for the game. They (politicians, not football fans) think it is the fault of voters, who don't appreciate what they do and what is done for them. How astonishing, they marvel, that anyone could fail to see how exciting and relevant politics are. To add insult to injury, they find it incredible that millions would rather vote someone out of the Big Brother house or on to the next round of *The X Factor* than choose a member of Parliament or a government, which is the only X factor they think matters.

Both sides of the argument have something going for them. Just as there are politicians who have done very nicely, thank you, out of public life, so there is a lack of appreciation for what has been achieved by politics down the years. Yet this is nothing new. Throughout history there has been a chasm between government and governed. Ordinary citizens have been mildly sceptical of politicians at best while for politicians the feeling has been mutual. Today the gap is wider than ever. What has changed to make the situation so much more critical and dangerous for our democracy? Read on to discover the sorry truth.

Elections used to generate enormous excitement. Here voters anxiously await the result of a 1931 poll when the big issue was whether the wearing of hats should be made compulsory. (National Library of New Zealand)

Much ado about nothing

Down the years, there have been countless political ideologies. Apathy has not been one of them. While whole libraries have been written about the various -isms – communism, capitalism and socialism, to name the most familiar – apathy, the great ideology of the non-political classes, has largely passed unobserved and unremarked.

Battalions of activists have marched in support of the most obscure causes yet never has there been even a small gathering for the non-cause of apathy. No shoe leather has been worn away marching for it and no one has gone hoarse addressing the issue without passion at public meetings or so much as whispering of it through a soft hailer at election times. The sad truth is, people are apathetic about apathy.

While campaigners have fought to the death for the right to vote, no one ever threw themselves under the hooves of the King's horse at the Derby because they wanted to stay at home on polling day. Or chained themselves to the railings of Downing Street or went on hunger strike for the right to avoid choosing their member of Parliament.

Never have thousands walked shoulder-to-shoulder from Hyde Park to Trafalgar Square chanting:

'What don't we want?'

'The vote!'

'When don't we want it?'

'Never!'

The dictionary definition of *apathy* is indolence, indifference and lack of feeling, so you wouldn't expect someone who fitted that specification to rise up and take arms against a sea of troubles or, frankly, even get agitated enough to scratch their bum over it.

But hang on a minute. Was there ever a member of the human race who didn't care about *anything*? Most of us are incredibly passionate, even furious, about a huge range of issues, from parking restrictions, to buses not turning up, to petty-fogging red tape, to stupid rules, to unfairness at work. . . the list goes on and on. And right at the top is the way the country is run and the behaviour of the people who claim to be running it. If you don't believe that, read the letters pages of newspapers, listen to radio phone-ins and scan the increasing number of internet blogs. There is a veritable tsunami of rage, an avalanche of anger, a volcano of passion out there.

Most of those accused of being apathetic because they don't

vote aren't apathetic at all. They just don't connect with the political process and consider it offers them nothing. Let us now confirm their prejudices.

Why vote? Why bother!

It has been said and, indeed, spray painted on at least one railway bridge that: 'if voting changed anything they would have abolished it'.

That may be the ultimate in cynicism but it is a pretty accurate reflection of how a growing number of people feel. And how far wrong can it be when we are governed by a party which four-fifths of those registered to vote didn't support?

But just because 80 per cent of the electorate, which is around thirty-seven million people, didn't get the government they wanted is no reason for any of them to take their bat home and swear they will never turn out for the team again. In fact, it is even more reason to take part in the next election so they can try to throw out the governing party (unless they have changed their mind in the meantime, which does sometimes happen). So there have to be other excuses for not voting. Here are a few of the common ones:

Politics is boring. True. Much of it inevitably is (all that poring over long, dull documents or listening to interminable speeches is never going to be exciting, is it?). In fact, if psychiatric analysis was called for, it should be those who find politics thrilling rather than those who find it a turn-off who ought to be on the couch.

Politicians are out of touch. Only partly true. Good MPs and councillors are in regular contact with constituents, so they know what they are saying and thinking and going through. But, at the same time, they do live in a rarefied world in which they mainly talk to people like themselves about subjects only people like them are interested in.

Voting is pointless. Again, partly true. The main parties agree about most big subjects, though often they pretend they don't. An MP who doesn't go along with the consensus is described as a rebel, even if the majority of the population agrees with them. Perhaps it would be more accurate to describe mainstream politicians as rebels as they are the ones out of step with much of public opinion.

My vote won't make a difference. Sadly, this is true for most people. If you live in a constituency with a big majority for one party, it doesn't matter a hoot which way you vote. Your vote will only make a difference if you live in a marginal seat.

I'm not interested in politics. OK, so you're not. But you're sure as hell interested in a whole lot of things which politics affects (see above) so don't confuse your lack of interest with contempt for the silly side of party politics.

They're all the same. Not true. There may be a public perception of an identikit politician but they are actually quite different. Look different, sound different, behave differently. Even over the expenses scandal, some MPs didn't take a penny while others ripped off the taxpayer for tens of thousands of pounds.

If you are not convinced by any of that, answer this question: Are you really happy to let other people decide who will take the decisions that affect your life? To decide how much you pay in tax, what sort of education your children will get, the hours you work and possibly even what you get paid, how fast you drive, where and when shops can open, whether our armed forces are sent to war, how the elderly are cared for and a zillion other things, big and little.

Yes, those boring, out-of-touch politicians who are so despised and vilified have the power to decide all that and much more while you – little old you – has the power to choose which of them will be given the power for the next few years. Sort of.

In the beginning. . .

Nobody set out to create Parliament. For centuries our forefathers were ruled by a king (and, very occasionally, a queen), who would from time to time summon the knights, barons and bishops to his palace for a primitive form of brainstorming away-day sessions.

The barons were supposed to represent the views of the people in their shires or towns although naturally they couldn't go as far as disagreeing with the King (if they lost their head and did, they would usually lose their head). But they got fed up with that so gradually and irreverently they began to meet of their own volition. They got so cocksure of themselves, sometimes they even invited the monarch to pop in.

Eventually this cosy arrangement went belly-up. Civil war broke out and poor old King Charles had *his* head lopped off. By then, Parliament had split in two, into a House of Lords and House of Commons (not because the members in it were common but after the word 'commune', meaning a small political group). With the death of Charles, Parliament had won.

It didn't last long. Within a few years, the monarchy was restored but it never again had the same power, so the supremacy of Parliament was established.

Origin of the specious

The House of Lords was, naturally enough, made up of lords whereas the House of Commons was composed of ordinary people. Well, to be precise, ordinary rich people, ordinary landowners, and ordinary younger sons of aristocrats. All elected by ordinary voters who owned property and were men. It was going to be a very long time before women made an appearance on the political scene.

Whereas Charles Darwin discovered the process of natural

selection, no one ever worked out the process of unnatural selection which resulted in an extremely narrow field from which politicians were chosen. Not that this made them bad people (not all of them, at least). There were actually some extraordinarily enlightened souls among them who did much to improve the lot of the common man (and sometimes woman).

With the industrial revolution came a new breed of ordinary chaps with designs on becoming MPs as ordinary factory owners joined the procession to Westminster. Political parties were created and the (elected) Commons became more important than the (unelected) Lords until eventually MPs completely overshadowed peers.

So a sophisticated political system developed while still only an extremely limited number of people (the aforementioned property-owning blokes) had the vote.

Inevitably there were growing demands for the franchise to be extended so that more men had the vote (no, not women, don't rush things). There was resistance to this from the ruling classes, who were not keen to let the teeniest fringes of power slip from their grasp. They were, after all, the Ones Who Mattered. The Natural Rulers with the God-given right to vote and be voted for because they owned property. And were men, of course.

Considering how vociferous politicians are today about the merits of democracy, it is strange to think that back then there was so much opposition to more people taking part in the democratic process.

You see, the problem with democracy is that it's fine in theory but the reality is that politicians don't always get the answers they want. Voters can, and do from time to time, behave in amazing ways. Like voting out governments. That's because although politicians are greedy for power and do all they can to hoard it like misers, ultimately power lies with the voters.

Just give me the facts

Right, wake up at the back. There are a few basic things you need to know. You might have some garbled version of them, picked up from that bigmouth in the pub or the old lady in the launderette or a long-haired guy in a tweed jacket at the bus stop, but you can be pretty sure what you heard is wrong.

To start at the beginning, Parliament is split in two, the House of Commons and the House of Lords. The Commons has 646 members, each one representing a constituency. The political party with the most MPs forms the government. The leader of that party is the Prime Minister.

The government proposes new laws and raises issues for Parliament to debate. It also puts into action the decisions Parliament makes. Over the years, governments have got more and more power and Parliament less and less. Yet still we don't vote directly for a government. In America, not only do voters choose the government (in the shape of the President) directly but their equivalent of Parliament, which is called Congress, has a lot more power than our parliament. That may sound more democratic yet still we go about boasting that we have the mother of parliaments, by which we mean not only that it is the oldest (not true, incidentally – Iceland's is older) but The Best. So here is a question for you to consider: If the UK parliament really is the best in the world, what does that say about the other parliaments scattered around the globe?

While pondering that tricky one, have a quick look at the House of Lords, the second chamber, the so-called Upper House. This may not be the oldest or the best legislature in the world but it sure has to be the weirdest. Though not as weird as it was until 1958.

Before then – a mere eleven years before man first walked on the moon, please note – all members of the House of Lords were hereditary, which meant the only reason they were there making our laws was because their great-great-great-great-great-great-grandfather had let his wife be the king's mistress or had won a joust in the queen's name or been the best sheep rustler in the Midlands. They had been made a baron or duke and so got to sit in the Lords and make the laws for everyone who hadn't let the king shag his wife or jousted for the queen or stolen huge flocks, and when he died his eldest son took over – to be followed by his son and so on down the centuries.

It was sons only. Daughters got no look in. If a peer had left no male heir, his brother or nephew or another male relative took over the title.

It was only in 1958, with the creation of life peers, that the first woman sat in the Lords. Life peers are selected by the Prime Minister or other party leader and remain in Parliament for the rest of their lives but the title dies with them. What's more (hold on to your ermine hats, folks), WOMEN were allowed to become life peers. Yes, at last, after a mere 700 years, a woman was allowed to be a member of the House of Lords (she was Baroness Swanborough, if you're ever asked in a pub quiz).

Forty years later, there was still a majority of hereditary peers in the House, many of them rarely visiting Westminster, but in 1999 most were kicked out, so now all but ninety-two members of the Lords are life peers. Still not elected but at least selected by someone who was, rather than by an accident of birth (and, with the way the aristocracy behaved, it often was an accident).

There have been several attempts to reform the Lords with the intention of making all (or most) of its members elected (which would give voters another election not to participate in). But the Upper Chamber is composed of people with huge experience not just of Parliament but all sorts of subjects, which the Commons lacks. So it's not all bad.

And that's enough facts for now.

Voting: A first step

With your appetite hopefully whetted for a bit of democracy, it's time for some D-I-Y. This is all you have to do:

1. Register to vote (a form comes to every household every year – fill it in and send it back). No stamp required.
2. Turn up at your polling station on election day (or you can do it by post).
3. Mark an X against the name of the candidate you want.

That's all. Easy, isn't it?

Actually, not everyone has the right to vote. You can't if you are under eighteen, not a British, Irish or Commonwealth citizen, a member of the House of Lords (although they can vote in local elections) or if you are in prison. The Queen does have a vote, but she hasn't been known to exercise it. Surely *she* can't be apathetic.

The chosen few

In America you get to vote for just about everyone from the President down to the local dog-catcher. In Switzerland, they allow votes on all sorts of trivial issues, as they do in California.

But in the UK, when it comes to national politics, we are only allowed to vote for our Member of Parliament presumably on the principle that we have the Mother of Parliaments and, as everyone knows, Mother knows best.

This system is known as representative democracy. We elect our representatives and they do what we want them to. Or, as it turns out, what they want to do. They believe we have given them the right to act in our best interests. This is clearly an extension of the Victorian idea that children should be forced to eat Brussels sprouts and take cod liver oil because it was good for them. And that they should be seen and not heard – the political equivalent being that voters should vote and then keep quiet for the next five years.

The party with most MPs forms the government and the government is entrusted to run the country. That is the theory and it seemed to work well enough for centuries, though that might be looking back through rose-tinted spectacles. Today things are different. The age of deference is over. We don't trust MPs to do what is best any longer though they still think they can carry on feeding us sprouts, cod liver oil, unpopular wars, higher taxes and trillions of pounds in bail-outs for fat-cat bankers.

We are kept well away from the action because we aren't allowed to directly choose the people who take the important decisions. We don't vote for the Prime Minister, for a start. You might think that is what you are doing at a general election, but it isn't. That has been particularly clear since Gordon Brown became PM. The only people who voted for him at the 2005 general election were 24,278 in Kirkcaldy & Cowdenbeath, his constituency. He became Labour leader and so Prime Minister without a vote from anyone else. Not even in the Labour Party, as his henchmen had taken any possible rivals out and had them shot (figuratively speaking).

No one votes for government ministers. The Prime Minister appoints them and fires them when he feels like it. Most ministers have at least been elected as MPs but there is a growing trend for individuals who have never been elected to anything to be plucked up by the Prime Minister and made a minister, with a seat in the House of Lords.

No one votes for the civil servants who actually run the country. And while we do vote for our local councillors, the council officers who do just about anything that matters are not elected. Nor are judges, police chiefs, the people who run hospitals and schools, the chairman and top executives at the BBC or anyone who is in charge of any of the hundreds of quangos and other public bodies.

So the chances are that the vote you cast at a general election, that corner-stone of democracy, will be given to a backbench MP with no power or a member of a party not in power. In other words, it doesn't really amount to a hill of refried beans. Unless you are one of those lucky 24,278 folk in Kirkcaldy & Cowdenbeath.

How to be an MP: a fantasy

1. Wait till you turn eighteen.
2. Join a political party.
3. Do a huge amount of crawling, buttering up and soothing of party members' egos.
4. Fight off all challengers with a mixture of charm, native cunning and brutality.
5. Then, when you have been selected as the candidate, all you have to do is win the election.

Easy it isn't yet there are many, many times more people who devote large chunks of their life to trying to be an MP than ever become one. And if you are selected as a candidate and fail to win and are bonkers enough to want to stand again, you have to go through another five years of knocking on doors and sitting in brain-numbing meetings before you lose again. Mad or what? But whatever you think of politicians, you have to give them an A for effort and persistence.

Heartbreaking footnote: You can't be an MP if you are a civil servant, an undischarged bankrupt, a member of the clergy, police or armed forces, a prisoner serving more than a year in jail or if you have been found guilty of electoral fraud (though that doesn't include lying to voters).

Begging for it

Politicians don't hang about when it comes to trawling for votes. Most of them send a card to constituents who reach the grand old age of eighteen It says: 'Happy Birthday!' What it means is: 'Now you can vote! So vote for *me*!' This is a wasted plea, as the other parties will have sent a similar card. And, honestly, can you imagine voting for someone simply because they sent you a birthday card? On that basis, you might as well vote for your granny.

MPs and councillors spend a considerable part of their lives showing their faces to the local electorate, turning up wherever voters are gathered (school fetes, public meetings), getting their names in the papers (today they write blogs, too), leading local campaigns and so on.

Yet very few people vote on the basis of who their MP is. They go for a particular party or the leader of that party (as if it were a presidential election). How frustrating is it for a good constituency MP from Party A who has done a lot for the people he represents to have many of them vote for Party B because they think that party's leader is nicer than the leader of Party A? But that's how it is, folks.

Power drunk on Monarch-lite

One of the incredible things about this country is that we have got into the twenty-first century and still have a monarch on the throne. While other countries got rid of theirs, chopping off their heads or killing them in other frightful ways, or allowed them to carry on with no powers or formal role in government, relegating them to living in a council flat, riding around on a bike, ours still have a selection of palaces, hordes of flunkies waiting on their every whim and, more relevantly, a place in the way we are governed.

Certainly the Queen doesn't throw her weight around like Henry VIII (and what a weight he had to throw around) but she remains the figurehead at the apex of our political system. We have what is called a constitutional monarchy.

Her Majesty can be seen once a year in all her finery arriving at a special entrance to the House of Lords in her horse-drawn carriage for the State Opening of Parliament. She solemnly reads out the Queen's Speech, which is actually what the Prime Minister has written about the government's plans for the coming months. She describes it as 'My government'. Not The People's government, please note. Which explains the reactionary mentality at the core of the British political system.

The monarch is only pretending to be in charge but taxpayers still have to pick up an annual £40 million bill for maintaining all those butlers, grooms and palaces. For a couple of hours' work a year, that equates to around £20 million an hour. Good money, eh? No wonder she hasn't swapped it for a job in the City.

To be fair, the Queen also sees the Prime Minister once a week for a chat. He comes to her, naturally, and explains what he is up to in her name. From time to time, learned professors and not-so-learned commentators get terribly excited discussing what powers Her Majesty would have if there were a Great Crisis, such as a hung Parliament when no one won an election with a working majority.

That could be when she comes into her own and decides on a whim who will be Prime Minister. Sadly, she has shown no inclination to indulge in this constitutional fun. Nor has she been tempted to be rebellious when it comes to her task of signing every new Act of Parliament before it can become law. For whatever agonies it requires to get a Bill through the Commons and Lords, however many hours of debate there have been before the final vote, it still doesn't become law until Her Majesty appends her name to it. With that power – the only real one she has – you might have thought she would occasionally say, 'No. Sorry. I don't like this. Afraid I'm not going to sign. Go away and think again.' But she has never done anything like that, no matter how much she disagrees with a new law. No, not even the ban on fox hunting.

So what we have in this country is Monarch-lite. Which may be something of a cop-out but is still more agreeable than being ruled over by President Blair or Thatcher.

I'm in charge!

As everyone knows, the person really in charge is the Prime Minister, a post which has existed for almost 300 years, though there is not an exact date as there was never a moment when the King or Parliament said, 'Hey, here's a good idea, let's have someone who is head of the government and let's call him the Prime Minister!' The job just evolved, like so much else to do with British government.

In theory, there are rules about what the Prime Minister can and can't do, and how he (or she) should do it. In practice, he can pretty well do what he likes. And Prime Ministers increasingly do. They appoint ministers and fire them and tell them what to do, if they can be bothered. They run their parties, which gives them pretty much control over who is chosen as MPs, despite the lip service paid to local democracy. They can declare war, negotiate international treaties and swan around the world posing as a statesman.

On top of all that, Prime Ministers have the power of patronage. Patronage means they grant favours to those who support them. Just like in olden times when the King would give land, titles or jobs to his favourites. The modern equivalents are a seat in the House of Lords, a government job, chairmanship of a quango or various other kinds of largesse. Legally there is a distinction between patronage and bribery – the PM is not allowed to grant favours, such as a peerage, to someone who has paid for it. Hence the furore when people around Tony Blair became embroiled in the Cash for Honours scandal.

Life isn't always fun and frolics for a Prime Minister. He can be taunted, humiliated and ultimately ignominiously dumped by his colleagues or the electorate. But it's the job they all aspire to because, if you are power crazy, you are desperate to be where ultimate power lies.

Subject or citizen

But enough about kings, queens and prime ministers. Let's talk about you.

You may not have lost much sleep over the question 'Am I a subject or a citizen?' But a lot of blood has been spilt and much fury generated in answering it.

A subject is someone subservient to the monarch. Someone who does what they are told, pays their taxes yet has no rights. A citizen on the other hand has the right to vote, to be tried fairly by a court and to have their opinions considered by their rulers.

That makes all of us in the UK citizens (although we are technically subjects of the Queen, even if she can't boss us around – a Very British Compromise).

We don't have an Absolute Monarchy (that was got rid of by Magna Carta in 1215) but we don't have Absolute Democracy either, as we can't elect our head of state. And we aren't Absolutely Free, as we give up that right in return for the protection that society provides.

If thinking about all that makes your head hurt, let's put it simply. The UK isn't a country of Absolutes. It is composed of compromises because everything has been decided gradually during years of argument between two sides who eventually met somewhere around the middle. And a jolly good thing, too.

Nations with extreme political systems always end in disaster and collapse. Those who despise the way we run our affairs should try the alternatives.

It helps that we are an island race and have been around for centuries, giving us the time and lack of space to work out how we will be governed. Unlike that brash young upstart the United States or our European neighbours, who were created through bloody revolutions, we have never recognised the need for a written constitution. There is a lot of unwritten stuff around, though, based on the idea that our society functions because citizens agree to be bound by the laws made in their name.

The theory is that we get something out of this arrangement, as the legal system and courts are there to uphold our rights and duties as citizens. They are supposed to be on our side and not to enforce the diktats of Parliament, which they have done quite a lot in recent years. The judges who stand up to the excesses of ministers quite often get a kicking in the press afterwards but thank God they still believe in basic British rights, even if the government doesn't.

People v Parliament

Our parliamentary system grew out of a desire for the people to have more say in how things are run. The trouble is an increasing number of people believe most MPs, all political parties and certainly the government couldn't give a hoot about what we think. All they want is our vote at election time, just like some dirty old man who is only after one thing.

There are times when people do rise up. They did over the unfair poll tax in 1990 and played a major part in the downfall of Margaret Thatcher. They did when Tony Blair wanted to take the country to war in Iraq and millions marched in protest. And hundreds of thousands of the least likely protestors congregated in Parliament Square to object to banning hunting.

Yet did all of them, energised and united at what they saw as bad government, use their votes wisely at the previous election? Or, indeed, use their votes at all?

Sometimes an individual has a huge impact, takes on the might of ministers and beats them, or at least makes them rethink. Look at Joanna Lumley's fight to allow the Gurkhas to settle in this country or Bob Geldof battling for the world's starving with Live Aid.

The relationship between people and Parliament is a lot more than occasional flashes of inspiration from celebrities. The whole point of Parliament is that MPs are given the authority to act on our behalf, so we are entitled to expect them to act in our best interests. With considered thought, intelligent debate, honesty and integrity before they pass new laws that will affect our lives.

If that isn't going to happen, the laws might as well be made by the loud bloke in the pub or the old dear who keeps 171 cats and thinks ballroom dancing is the answer to world peace.

Trust me, I'm a politician

Until recently estate agents, journalists and second-hand car salesmen were at the bottom of the pile when it came to public trust. Now politicians are lower than any of them. An opinion poll at the height of the expenses scandal showed that a pathetic 13 per cent of people trusted politicians to tell the truth while 82 per cent thought they did not, the worst result in polling history.

This is different from the normal cynicism we need to survive. After all, who really believes that 'the cheque is in the post' or 'I don't usually do this on a first date'? We are dubious about official statistics and sceptical about promises, especially from the chairmen of football clubs and politicians.

What is really staggering is that we let them get away with it, time after time. We wouldn't take it from our colleagues, a holiday company, a supermarket or the milkman so why, when it comes to political promises, do we shrug our shoulders and think we can't do anything about it? We can. We are THE PEOPLE. They are the politicians. *We* are the masters. Or at least, we ought to be.

The trouble is, too many of The People turn away, think they can't change anything and so don't hold politicians to account. How supine is that? Would anyone ignore burglars, vandals or bank robbers because there is no point in making them behave? So why are so many people happy to leave in power the people who have let us down time after time?

Part of the answer is that politics is run like a secret society with its own weird rules, procedures and even language. It dissuades outsiders – i.e. the vast majority of ordinary law-abiding citizens – from taking part, though it says it is desperately keen for them to vote.

So if you are thinking of joining the Apathy Party, it's time to grasp some basic facts about our political system. Not that they are guaranteed to make you more likely to vote. In fact, they may convince you voting is a serious waste of your precious time. But we hope not.

The only dogs allowed in Parliament, according to myth, are Cavalier King Charles spaniels. Here the MP for Barking East relaxes before a late-night debate. (David Seymour)

Facts and fictions

If you are thinking of voting there are some elementary things you ought to know about how Parliament and the political system works. Though ignorance has never been a barrier to voting (sometimes it seems a positive advantage.)

On the next few pages you will find the most basic facts. They are not compulsory reading. So have a look if you feel like it, or skip them and come back later when there is nothing on the telly or you pick this book up in the loo.

If and when you do read them, you will find some things which will amaze you and some which will give you a bit of a giggle.

What is Parliament?

It is a talking shop stuffed with people who like the sound of their own voices and who never miss an opportunity to listen to themselves, though they don't seem as keen to hear what anyone else has to say. At least, that is what it seems like to the outside world.

But it is also the place where government ministers come from, where they announce what they are doing about running the country and where they are held to account by MPs who aren't part of the government. All that is done in your name, as MPs are elected by The People. Sounds impressive, even if many Britons are no longer impressed, but you have to admit you can see why our parliamentary system gets talked up big as being the exemplary way to govern a country. Especially if the alternative is some despot or dictator ordering everyone around and getting rid of those who don't like what he is doing.

It has never been as perfect as the theory suggests – it couldn't be when, by definition, a political system has to be run by politicians. A recent suggestion that non-politicians should be allowed to get involved is like suggesting that non-drivers should be let loose on the roads or plumbers take over from doctors – or, for that matter, doctors take over from plumbers. In recent years, a few ministers have been brought in from outside Parliament, having been given a peerage so they can sit in the Lords, but have had limited success.

The importance of Parliament has diminished as more power has been grabbed by ministers, particularly the Prime Minister, and the black art of spin has taken over from traditional parliamentary activities. Although government announcements are still formally made in the House, most of them are leaked out in advance to friendly newspapers (the minister then goes on the radio or television but says he can't talk about it until Parliament has been told – a fatuous way to behave that insults voters' intelligence).

As for holding the government to account, MPs only manage to do that 0.00001 per cent of the time (approximate figure made up for effect by the authors, much as ministers make up impressive-looking statistics to suit their case). The government just bats away criticism or suggestions on the arrogant principle of 'We're in charge, you're just the opposition, so go take a running jump: we know what we're doing.' Tragically, too often they haven't a clue what they are doing and some time in the future they have to come back to the House to pretend they didn't mean it after all and no, they won't admit they got it wrong and the only reason they are now reversing what they did before is simply because. . . because. . . oh, go away and stop bothering us!

The Commons

Before we go any further, let's go back to basics. What exactly is this House of Commons that politicians are so proud of? The simplest way to explain it to a modern audience is as the next best thing to the Big Brother house for people who like to show off in public and will do almost anything to attract attention in the hope of not being voted out.

It is a sad fact, though, that more votes are cast during *Big Brother* than at a general election.

This is a cause of bewilderment to Members of Parliament, not only because they have an over-developed sense of self-importance but they don't properly understand public taste, though they pretend they do to make them appear populist and trendy.

They are baffled at why so many people will watch a reality show in which a group of eccentric characters sit around for hours talking rubbish. Surely viewers should be watching the Parliament Channel, when they can see a group of eccentric characters sitting around for hours talking gibberish.

The House of Commons does occasionally provide electrifying drama. Very, very occasionally. But if *EastEnders* only had one gripping plot every ten years, it wouldn't get millions tuning in night after night. There is a limited audience for a discussion of, say, amendment 19 to paragraph 117, clause 3, sub-clause (d) of the Weights and Measures (Wales) Bill – probably restricted to those who are particularly interested in how many grains of basmati rice there should be in a half-kilo packet or some such.

Not that anyone goes into politics because they want to sit for endless hours debating the minutiae of bureaucracy (that's why people go into the civil service) but that is what they do for much of the time because that is how laws are made. And making laws is what Parliament is about.

What is a law?

We all know the law says you can't drive at more than 30 miles an hour in a built-up area and you can't rob a bank (unless you are its chief executive, when you can help yourself to millions without fear of reprisals as long as you call it a bonus) and you shouldn't kill someone because he has run off with your wife. But these criminal laws are a fraction of the hundreds of thousands of laws that rule every bit of our lives.

There is almost nothing you can do that isn't governed by law. At work, at home, in the streets, affecting the things you buy, how your children are educated and your elderly relatives are looked after and on and on and on. As well as the main laws there are also thousands more regulations.

Some of these come from the European Union but still the great majority are the government's. And this Everest of law comes from Parliament.

Without laws, we would live in a state of anarchy. Imagine if we could choose whether to drive on the right or left of the road, to mention but one barmy idea. That doesn't mean, though, that all laws are necessary. In fact, most people would agree that a lot of them aren't.

Since Labour came to power in 1997, it has passed almost 4,000 new laws. Yes, four thousand. Even the Prime Minister would be hard pressed to name a tenth of them. In fact, that's a good idea – someone should ask him to.

Between politicians who feel they have to be seen to be doing something and civil servants who feel that is what God put them on this earth for, new laws erupt out of the Palace of Westminster like a gusher on an oil field.

Is that it?

Parliament does do other things apart from passing laws like a tourist with Delhi belly. There are those big set-piece occasions like the Budget and dramatic debates on controversial issues. Though the Commons is always capable of turning a drama into a disappointment, as listening to the Chancellor drone on every year about the economy usually is. He wades through interminable statistics which mean nothing to anyone except a few clever people in the City just to get to the bit where he announces there will be no change in income tax and a penny is going on a pint of beer. It might not do much to stir up the apathetic masses but it's a sure cure for insomnia.

Just as important as what goes on with official business is what MPs do. So let's deal with the question on so many lips nowadays: What has my bloody MP ever done for me?

The first thing to realise is that, whoever you voted for or even if you didn't vote, your MP is supposed to represent YOU. Yes, little old you. You can ask him or her for help and you won't be asked:

'Before we start, can I ask if you gave me your vote at the election? No? Then piss off, you sad loser.'

There must be times when they sort out someone's problems through gritted teeth, knowing they didn't get their vote or may even belong to another party, but they get on with it. They may have to battle against the local council which is run by their own party on behalf of the supporter of another party.

First and foremost, the job of every MP is to represent his or her constituents. Even the Prime Minister, the Foreign Secretary and other ministers turn up in a cold hall on a Friday night to listen to local people whingeing on about their housing problems or the street light that stays on after midnight shining into their bedroom window or the dog next door barking at all hours.

It is a wonderful image of British politics that the President of the USA can call to speak to the PM and be told he can't come to the phone because he is busy helping Miss Higginbottom sort out the problem with her mother's care worker. And, to be fair, Mrs Higginbottom senior's difficulties are just as important to her as the President's troubles are to him (and the world, possibly).

For a long time there was also a rather grand idea that anyone could go to the House of Commons, walk up to the desk in Central Lobby and ask to see their MP. If he was around, he would come through to see them.

How times change. Security is so tight nowadays that is almost impossible. Besides, MPs tend to have much busier diaries so are not free in the way they were when their main role was to wander about Westminster looking important and wondering where their next lunch was coming from. Sadly, the face-to-face meeting with an MP has been replaced by the email (try your MP's surname followed by their initial @ parliament.uk – as in churchillw@parliament.uk – but don't bother trying that particular one. Winston hasn't got the hang of emailing yet.)

The advantage of taking a problem to your MP is that, even if the general public views politicians with contempt, officials rarely do. A letter from you may get nowhere but one from your MP should get wheels turning.

If you are really lucky, your MP may even raise your case in the Commons. As in: 'Is the Prime Minister aware that my constituent Mr Salamander has been waiting two years to have his leaking roof repaired? Can he investigate the gross inefficiency of Plonker Council?' This is a particularly good ploy if the council is run by the opposition, as it gives the PM a chance to say this just goes to show what a mess the country would be in if they ran the government and not merely some tin-pot council.

You might never need to see or speak to your MP, might not even know what he looks like, but you can bet once an election is called he'll be all over you like a rash. It's like a husband who ignores his wife until he wants sex. Just as she should ask 'So why are you suddenly saying how nice I look?' you should ask your MP: 'So where have you been for the past four years, matey?'

Seconds out for the main bout

There are two images people have of the Commons chamber. One is of rows of empty green benches with one MP on his feet droning on while a handful of bored-looking members lounge around him. The other is of the House with every bench packed, ample bottom jammed up against ample bottom, MPs even squatting on the steps between the aisles while others stand just inside the doors. This is what it is like for the weekly top-of-the-bill joust between the Prime Minister and leader of the opposition when for thirty minutes they hurl insults at each other over the despatch box. Yes, it's Prime Minister's Questions, the modern equivalent of bear baiting and a less mucky version of wrestling in mud.

Since Parliament has been televised, other countries have taken to showing recorded highlights. Not because they are fascinated by British politics but because nowhere else in the world can you see such an incredible spectacle. They must think of it as some form of reality TV, instead of which it is un-reality politics.

The referee of this contest is the Speaker, who sits Buddha-like between the combatants on his throne until the noise from the baying hordes on the back benches becomes so dreadful he is forced to leap to his feet and desperately call out 'Order! Order!' followed by something like 'Honourable members must allow the leader of the opposition to be heard'. As if.

For the baying and heckling and shouting and provoking is part of the fun. How boring it would be if MPs sat there in silence, they reason, if they listened respectfully to what the leader of the opposing party said, and then muttered, 'Good point, old chap, damned fine point. And well put, if I might say so.' Instead they jeer and barrack. What an example to set to any children who may be watching.

In case you have never seen PMQs and this brief account has whetted your appetite, here is how the ritual works. MPs don't ask proper questions such as 'Can the Prime Minister tell us why his education policy is a flop?' or 'Will the Prime Minister explain why our troops don't have enough equipment?'. Instead, they almost always ask the same question: 'Can the Prime Minister list his engagements today?' If that was the end of it, PMQs would be incredibly dull. The Prime Minister would spend thirty minutes saying over and over again: 'I had meetings with ministerial colleagues and later today I will be having more meetings.' But of course no one is interested in what he is doing, unless he planned to scale the Big Ben tower. What the questioner is after is to surprise the PM with his real thrust, hoping he succeeds in tying him in knots trying to reply. Actually, he doesn't because prime ministers don't attempt to answer difficult questions, contenting themselves with abusing the party opposite and, on a good day, the questioner himself.

This ritual only applies to opposition MPs. Every alternate question comes from a government backbencher and includes the political equivalents of 'Is the Prime Minister aware that he is the most saintly person to set foot in this country since St Augustine but far better looking?'. Wow, that's a tough one, isn't it?

Quite why loyal MPs are allowed to bowl such pathetic slow balls no one outside Parliament can understand. The Speaker should ban anyone who does that from asking another question for a year. Or ever.

The leader of the opposition is allowed to ask six questions. Yes, six. This gives the Prime Minister six opportunities to attack the leader of the opposition, instead of answering, and to boast how well the government is doing. It is so rare for a PM to actually give a straight answer that you might suspect it is against parliamentary rules. (How wonderful it would be if the Speaker leapt to his feet and demanded that the Prime Minister withdraw what he has just said because he *answered the question*. Cries of 'Shame!' from opposition benches.)

You might think that ignoring real questions and being asked patsy ones by your own side makes Prime Minister's Questions a doddle for the PM. Far from it. It is a nerve-wracking occasion. Harold Wilson used to steady himself with a large brandy beforehand and Harold Macmillan got so nervous he was frequently sick – though never in the House, thankfully.

A vanishing breed

Apart from those weekly half-hours of PMQs, any viewer who happens to tune in to Parliament at any other time – or a tourist who drops into the public gallery to see British Democracy At Work

– will immediately notice one thing about MPs. There are hardly any on display. Acres and acres of green benches are there, certainly, but Members of Parliament are as rare as a cuckoo in winter.

This raises an obvious question. If Parliament is so vitally important, why are the majority of MPs absent so much of the time? You can imagine what they would say if they visited a school and found 95 per cent of the pupils absent.

If the TV cameras stay focused on the chamber at the end of Prime Minister's questions, you can see the migration happening. Those packed benches empty before you can shout 'Order'. Where could they all have gone? Six hundred MPs can't suddenly be desperate for a loo break or have just remembered an urgent appointment with a constituent. If *they* can't be bothered hanging around to hear what is being said, why should anyone else? They get paid for it, after all.

So let us follow them out of the Commons chamber and see what our elected representatives are up to.

Ministers will be running their ministries, organising civil servants, holding meetings and getting on with the other rituals of government. They do have a proper job, after all.

But what of the other 500-odd MPs? Where are they?

Look! There's one of them. There! In the tea room. My God, he's *drinking tea*. And *talking to someone*. Let's sidle up and see if we can hear what they are saying. Oh, how dull. She's another MP and they are discussing an early day motion they are planning to put down on the order paper next week.

Right, let's keep looking for the skivers. Hey, those could be some. There's half-a-dozen sauntering brazenly through that door. OK – let's walk in there ourselves and catch them at what they are doing. Could be playing poker or having a snooze. Whoops. It's a meeting of a select committee. They are grilling some ashen-faced civil servant. Better back out of the room quietly.

Aha! May have more luck here. We are in the new Portcullis House office block. Sure to find MPs having sex with their secretaries over the desk or watching porno movies or organising their next freebie holiday – sorry, fact-finding visit to the Bahamas – at taxpayers' expense.

Well, what a disappointment. We've been into several rooms and no illicit sex, no dirty films and no sneaky behaviour of any kind. They are all writing letters or holding meetings or preparing speeches.

Yes, the truth is that MPs lead incredibly dull lives. There are a few who misbehave but there can't be many workplaces where someone doesn't occasionally break the rules.

And that is what the Palace of Westminster is. A workplace. The difference between it and other offices or factories is that the 646 key people employed there only got the job because they were voted in. And can be voted out.

The crux of the problem

One reason voters think so little of MPs is that while they don't see the conscientious work they perform, they do see the nonsense side of politics. They are on public display shouting abuse at each other and behaving like four-year-olds let loose at a party with jelly.

When they appear on radio or television, they are either argumentative or evasive or both (this is a brilliant trick and is only comparable to the person who can be passionate and apathetic at the same time). They defend the indefensible. They are supinely loyal and treacherously disloyal, occasionally at the same time – another extraordinary feat of twisted character. But all these faults are trivial compared with the big accusation made against MPs.

The lie of the land

OK, let's get the old joke out of the way: How can you tell when a politician is lying? When his lips are moving.

Actually, it is rather more complicated than that. The thing is, not many politicians deliberately lie. (A small number do but they are psychopaths and with luck will eventually go to jail.) What is really scary about most politicians isn't that they knowingly tell lies but that they believe what they are saying, even when to the rest of the world what they are saying is patent rubbish. The proof that deep down they know the truth is that once ministers are out of office, they quite often say the complete opposite of what they had said with total conviction – and belief – when they were in power.

The most blatant example of this conviction politics (in which a politician is convinced he is right, even when all sense and evidence shows he isn't) is Tony Blair's insistence that Saddam Hussein had weapons of mass destruction so invading Iraq was right. His critics say Blair was lying. But was he? He was certainly telling a lie yet he was utterly convinced it was the truth. Does that make it a lie or not? The jury is still out, at the time of writing, so this deep intellectual riddle goes down with similar conundrums such as How many angels can dance on the head of a pin? and Is this the way to Amarillo?

Another impossible question is: Who are the bigger liars – politicians or journalists? Consider this situation: An MP tells a reporter something 'off the record' which the reporter prints or says on air. Because there is a hostile public reaction, the politician immediately denies that any such thing happened or is likely to happen. The 'story' is untrue and the journalist is accused of making it up, which means lying. But it isn't his lie, it's the politician's.

This is an occupational hazard for journalists, who regularly

hear a politician say something in private and shortly afterwards
hear him say the opposite in public. Is the assumption that what
was said in private is what the MP really thinks? Or is it what he
wants the reporter to think? Which is the lie and which the truth?
And does the politician know?

None of this is an excuse for the way MPs and their acolytes
behave but it does give ammunition to those who are convinced
that voting for such duplicitous liars is a waste of time and an insult
to their intelligence.

Chamber potty

On the night of 10 May 1941, the Luftwaffe succeeded where
Guy Fawkes had failed. It bombed the Palace of Westminster and
destroyed the Commons chamber.

That didn't stop them talking, naturally. They evicted the peers
from the House of Lords and moved in there for the duration of
the war.

A problem then faced the wartime Prime Minister, Winston
Churchill (as if he didn't have enough on his plate already). The
chamber had not been large enough to provide seats for all MPs, as
their number had grown considerably since Parliament was rebuilt in
the middle of the nineteenth century. Should the new one be bigger?

Churchill decided it shouldn't. Not to save building materials
which could be put to better use in the war effort (though not many
tanks were equipped with green leather seats) but he wanted to
preserve the intimate nature of the Commons chamber.

That is why when all MPs are present, some have to sit on
the steps in the aisles while others stand at the back opposite the
Speaker, behind the white line known as the bar (not to be confused
with the nineteen other bars in the Palace of Westminster).

This makes for the impression at moments of high passion –

genuine or manufactured – that the Commons is a bear pit. The sound is deafening as MPs shout, jeer and cheer. It is more like a primary school playground than a reverential chamber where the work of governing is solemnly carried on.

For more than 500 years, the dominant colour in the Commons has been green but no one knows for sure why. It makes the House look decidedly less grand than the Lords, where peers luxuriate on red leather.

It has been suggested that green symbolises the bounty of nature and fertility, though what that has to do with members of Parliament is anyone's guess.

Even pottier

Politicians pride themselves on having their fingers on the pulse, knowing what The People think and want, and having a visionary view of a better future. This is an extraordinary delusion for a group of people whose working environment was out of date in the nineteenth century.

The Houses of Parliament – actually called the Palace of Westminster because monarchs once lived on this site – were built in the middle of the nineteenth century, which is quite recent in terms of British history. But they look a lot older because they were designed in the Gothic style, which the French invented 700 years earlier and which had been out of fashion for 300 years before being revived to replace the parliamentary buildings burnt down in a freak fire (it certainly wasn't caused by a heated debate).

What goes on inside that strange exterior is just as much a throwback to bygone centuries, even though attempts have been made in the past few years to modernise procedures. They have their own language – rather like dysfunctional twins – extraordinary rituals and a bizarre style of dress for officials. If men walked

around in black tights and frilly cuffs anywhere except the Houses
of Parliament, they would be arrested.

Wigs were worn by the Speaker until Betty Boothroyd became
the first woman to hold that post and didn't want her coiffure messed
up by a smelly old mop of dead hair. Parliamentary officers still wear
them as well as the rest of the outfits that go back at least 200 years.

MPs used to wear swords until one accidentally caught the wig
of another member.

The most complicated rituals concerned hats. Silk top hats were
compulsory (although the first Labour leader, Keir Hardie, insisted
on a cloth cap to show he was a working man and not a toff) in the
Commons chamber but not when entering or leaving it, or when
speaking. So an MP would remove his hat when going in to the
chamber, put it on when he was sitting down, take it off when he
got up to speak, put it on again when he sat down and take it off
when he left the chamber. Are you keeping up with this? He had to
take his hat off when he went to vote but put it on to cast his vote.
It is not clear if a vote cast bare-headed would not count: it would
be a novel way to abstain.

Nowadays hats are not worn in the chamber, although until
1998 an MP had to put on a top hat – kept for the purpose – if he
wanted to raise a point of order.

There are still quite strict rules about dress, as you would
expect in what remains very much a gentlemen's club. Male MPs
have to wear jackets and ties. When the black MP Bernie Grant
wore a traditional Ghanaian cotton robe for the State Opening
of Parliament, there was uproar. But he was following in a
noble tradition. Oliver Cromwell was condemned for wearing 'a
plain cloth suit made by an ill country tailor and a hat without
a hatband'. Presumably not having a hatband in the seventeenth
century was the rebellious equivalent of wearing African dress
three centuries later.

Then there is the language. MPs are not referred to by name but are called 'the honourable member' or 'the member for West Wittering' or 'my honourable friend' (even when the speaker hates him). Until recently an MP who had served in the forces was called 'gallant' (even if he never saw action) and one who was a lawyer was 'learned' (even if he was totally stupid).

Using what is termed unparliamentary language is a serious offence, so MPs cannot say another member is lying or drunk, even if they are lying or drunk or both. They are not allowed to call each other a blackguard, coward, git, guttersnipe, hooligan, rat, swine, stool pigeon or traitor.

Other rules ban the reading of newspapers, magazines, letters or BlackBerrys in the chamber. Eating and drinking are forbidden, too, but weren't always. In fact, at one time debates were carried on against the background noise of oranges being sucked and nuts being cracked.

Smoking is banned in the chamber but this is not a consequence of the recent crackdown on having a fag in public places. Amazingly, smoking has not been allowed since 1693, probably the first ban in the world and a rare case of MPs leading through example. They are allowed to take snuff, though, and it is still provided at public expense.

With the exception of guide dogs, canine friends are not allowed. There is a theory that Cavalier King Charles spaniels are exempt from this ban but it has never been put to the test. In any case, the interbreeding of this variety makes it more suitable for the House of Lords.

One final quirk of our strange parliamentary system. When Bills become Acts of Parliament, they are still inscribed in Norman French, a language not commonly spoken in this country for nearly a thousand years. Not many know what '*Sooit baille aux communes*' or '*A ceste Bille les seigneurs sont assentus*' mean, but that is the point.

Anyone who doesn't speak Norman French, keep a silk top hat in the cupboard under the stairs or look good in a wig just isn't One Of Us.

The Speaker

You wouldn't think a job which had led to the violent deaths of seven of its holders would have many takers. But the last election for Speaker of the House of Commons attracted ten runners.

In any other place, the person who held this post would be called the chairman, because that is what he (or, in one instance, she) does – chairs sessions of the Commons and desperately struggles to keep order. But he is called the Speaker because, long ago, he had to speak on behalf of MPs. Which is why so many had their heads chopped off. Presumably if an MP spoke out of turn and the King demanded to know who said that, the errant member could point at the Speaker and say: 'I cannot tell a lie, Sire, it was him!'

Nowadays things have moved on. Although the last Speaker, Michael Martin, acted like a shop steward for MPs, defending their outrageous and in some cases unlawful expenses claims and doing all he could to keep them secret, he became the first for 314 years to be sacked. He wasn't executed, though. He was given a peerage and a large pension instead.

Until recently, the Speaker wore very strange clothes – strange not only for the twenty-first century but for the nineteenth. These included a wig, frilly cuffs, knee breeches, silk stockings and pointy shoes with buckles. How was anyone supposed to take him seriously?

The current Speaker has chosen to wear a business suit with a black robe – similar to the garb of schoolmasters in posh schools. And still no one takes him seriously.

Because so many Speakers in bygone times lost their heads and Parliament never misses an opportunity to do something inane that is rooted in history, when a new one is elected a charade is performed in which he is 'dragged', resisting, to the Speaker's chair as if the last thing in the world he wanted to do was occupy it. If that was so, why did he spend months campaigning for the job?

Actually, events in the final days of Michael Martin showed that today it is a lot harder to drag a Speaker *out* of the chair.

The work of the Speaker is as much a routine as that of the man who winds up Big Ben. Each day before the House sits, he (the Speaker, that is, not the man who winds up Big Ben) processes – i.e. walks slowly – through Central Lobby into the Commons chamber attended by various flunkies while a policeman calls 'Hats off, strangers'.

Apart from shouting 'Order! Order!' a lot, the Speaker's main job is deciding which MPs to call in a debate. So members put a lot of effort into trying to 'catch the Speaker's eye'. This was particularly difficult when Sir John Trevor was in the chair in the 1690s. He was so cross-eyed it was hard to work out who he was looking at.

The Speaker has one of the best homes in the country, a magnificent set of apartments in the tower which houses Big Ben, just below the clock. Though he must be kept awake by the bongs ringing out every quarter of an hour.

Home, sweet home

There is one address in Westminster which is even more sought after than the flat under the big clock: 10 Downing Street. However, the chequered past of this short cul-de-sac off Whitehall is far from illustrious. It was originally a bog, then the repository of some shanty shacks before being bought by Sir George Downing, a traitor, spy and, worse still, property developer. Setting the standards for developers down the ages, he stuck up various buildings as cheaply as possible with inadequate foundations, even having mortar lines drawn on the houses so it looked as if they had evenly spaced brickwork.

The area was unpleasantly sleazy, with gin palaces and brothels infesting it. After a history of bogs, dodgy development and red-light district, could it sink any lower? Yes, it could. It became home to the Prime Minister.

The current No 10 (which used to be No. 5) was created in Charles II's time by knocking three houses together, much to the fury of the neighbour at the back, the Countess of Lichfield. This was a particular problem because this aristocratic NIMBY complained to her daddy, who happened to be the king. He suggested she should 'speak to Mr Surveyor, who will build up your wall as high as you please'. The 'Mr Surveyor' he referred to was a jobbing architect called Sir Christopher Wren, who presumably was expected to build up the wall on his days off from designing St Paul's Cathedral. Calling Wren 'Mr Surveyor' is like referring to Einstein as 'Mr Sums' – but that's monarchy for you.

The early tenants of No. 10 were a succession of private residents, the last being a Mr Chicken who moved out in the early 1730s (to cross the road?). The new inhabitant was Sir Robert Walpole, the First Lord of the Treasury, who later moonlighted as the first Prime Minister. Nearly 300 years later, even though no one is quite sure what the First Lord of the Treasury does, that is what it says on the brass plaque on the door to No 10, next to the one reading 'No Junk Mail or Circulars'.

Under George II's Right-To-Buy scheme, Walpole was offered No 10 but he declined, insisting that it should become the home of future prime ministers. How different Sir Robert's noble gesture was from that of current MPs, many of whom have made large sums of money by buying and selling homes thanks to subsidy from the taxpayer.

One Prime Minister who made a particular impact at No. 10

was Benjamin Disraeli. He is remembered today as many things – statesman, businessman, author. A lesser-known interest of his has been overlooked by historians – his fascination with plumbing. In 1877 he splashed out £150 3s 6d on a bath with hot water. Not to be outdone, three years later his great rival, William Gladstone, had electricity and phones installed at an astonishing cost of £1,555 5s. That is £75,134.13 in today's money, a lot of dosh for a tenant with no security of tenure.

One drawback of living in 10 Downing Street – apart from the heavy security introduced over the past twenty years, which makes getting the milk delivered such a pain – is that you may not get on with your neighbour. No. 11 is where the Chancellor of the Exchequer lives.

Downing Street remains both the home and office of the Prime Minister, although he now lives above No. 11, the flat above No. 10 being considered too small. But Margaret and Denis Thatcher found it suited them well enough and she enjoyed 'living above the shop', which befits the daughter of a shopkeeper. As well as running the country, she insisted on cooking her husband's dinner every evening. As there was rarely anything in the fridge, she boasted: 'There was nothing I didn't know how to do with an egg.' A statement which over-excited the fevered imaginations of some members of her Cabinet.

Women and other rare species

Mention of Mrs Thatcher brings us neatly to the subject of women. She famously said: 'I don't think there will be a woman Prime Minister in my lifetime', although she was leader of her party two years later and PM four years after that. So Conservative MPs didn't choose her because of her brilliant ability to foresee the future.

There are few white-collar occupations which women have so struggled to get into, get accepted in and get on in as politics. They didn't have the vote until after World War I and even then few of them made it to Westminster. When Mrs Thatcher first became an MP in 1959 she was one of only nineteen women in the Commons.

Everything was weighted against them. There were hardly even any ladies' loos, although there was a gun range for the chaps to practise shooting. Much has changed but the Houses of Parliament are still an overwhelmingly male-orientated place in which women manage to get on through tokenism rather than by acceptance of their abilities.

There is criticism about the failure of women to get on in all sorts of other occupations, from the City to the media to academia, but the difference with politics is that politicians are supposed to represent the people. And half the population is female.

At the 2005 general election, 128 women were elected, the highest ever number. That is one in five, so still nowhere near being properly representative of their sex's proportion in the population. Yet women are crucial to the result of elections. They are stronger supporters of the Conservative Party than men and, in fact, if women didn't have the vote, Britain would have had almost continuous Labour government since 1945. Women were big backers of Tony Blair, though, and played a major part in his victories.

So women who don't vote aren't just letting down the memory of the suffragettes who fought – and died – to get them enfranchised, they are not playing their key part in deciding who rules the country.

Women aren't the only under-represented group in Parliament. Ethnic minorities clearly are, too, and need particular resilience to make their way in politics. Is it any surprise that so many of them are reluctant to vote?

The other section of the population which finds it an uphill struggle to get on at Westminster is that shrinking section of British society, the working class. When Labour was in its infancy, there would usually be a smattering who made it to Westminster via the trade union movement. Today that is a rare route to take. The path to Westminster is far more likely to be through university and a short internship working for an MP or a think-tank. A number of Labour MPs have been helped on their way by working for that populist newspaper the *Financial Times*.

In theory, we now have a classless society, rather like the Americans. In practice, the school you went to is more useful than anything. Nearly 60 per cent of the current parliamentary Conservative Party went to private school and fourteen of their 198 MPs were at Eton. Plenty of Labour and Lib Dem MPs went to private schools too, including Tony Blair and Harriet Harman.

The working class (at least, what remains of them) continue to vote Labour, but are not as committed as their parents and grandparents. The turn-out in strongly working-class constituencies falls and falls. But is it surprising? They increasingly feel that no one represents their interests in Parliament.

When is a Cabinet not a piece of furniture?

Before we leave Mrs Thatcher, here is one of the best Thatcher jokes, courtesy of *Spitting Image*. She is sitting down to dinner with her Cabinet and the waiter asks what she would like to eat. She says beef. 'And what about the vegetables,' asks the waiter. 'Oh, they'll have the beef, too,' replies Mrs T.

This not only demonstrates the contempt in which the Iron Lady held her closest colleagues but is cruelly accurate about the position of the senior ministers who form the Cabinet nowadays. These are the secretaries of state, who head up the major departments and whose traditional meeting every Tuesday while Parliament is sitting is supposed to be the key weekly session in the government of the country. Not for a long time has that been true.

In the same way that politicians don't listen to constituents, the

Prime Minister doesn't listen to the Cabinet. Most of them over the past quarter-century have hardly even bothered asking for their opinions. The exception was John Major, and look what a mess that got him into.

The bind for Cabinet members is that they have to support Cabinet decisions, however much they disagree with them, even if they voted against them (assuming they are allowed a vote) and even if they weren't at the Cabinet meeting. It must be particularly galling for dissidents if they learn about 'Cabinet decisions' from an announcement in the media and are then expected to publicly support them. This is how Tony Blair and his enforcers did things.

Lords above

If you think membership of the House of Commons comes from a narrow class, look at the composition of the House of Lords. The Lower House is positively all-encompassing by comparison. As we have pointed out already, until 1958 every ermined man jack of the Lords used to be there because he had been given land and favours by the king and in return was happy to provide troops for whatever military adventure the monarch might want to embark on.

It couldn't last. The ungrateful wretches soon got ideas above their station and decided to assert their independence. This they did by getting the King to sign Magna Carta, which is now considered to be about giving all British citizens freedom from oppression but was really aimed at letting rich, powerful barons avoid being bossed around by the rich, powerful monarch.

It took a very long time for the situation to change, as it always does in this country. 'Evolution not revolution' is our motto. The creation and rise of a second chamber, the House of Commons, gradually relegated the importance of the Lords.

We have already seen how the place went to rack and ruin in the twentieth century with the creation of life peers, who could be any rag, tag and retiring MP, and the admission of – horror of horrors! – women.

Poking fun at the Lords, sneering at the advanced average age of its members (well into their seventies for the current cohort of Tories) and mocking their fancy dress is easy but they do have some advantages.

For a start, you don't have to vote for them, which is a bonus to anyone who doesn't want to vote, though it turns fervent believers in democracy to an apoplectic rage. Peers also tend to work a fair bit harder than MPs and they have considerably more knowledge and experience than you find in their colleagues in the Commons.

Party leaders continue to insist that they will reform the Lords, though none has settled on how to do it. The trouble is, no Prime Minister is keen to lose his power of patronage, the ability to reward faithful time-servers with a job for life on the comfy red leather benches of the Upper House. Or even lose the ability to create a parliamentary seat for a mate by offering an MP a peerage if he (or she) would care to take the gentle stroll across Central Lobby to a life of bliss in the Lords.

There are other advantages in keeping the Peers' House as it is. For one thing, members don't get paid, which makes it cheaper to run than the Commons. They get an attendance allowance for each day they turn up, but as only around a third attend regularly, that's not expensive – or democratic, of course.

The number of peers has been tumbling – from more than 1,200 in 1999 to around 700 now – as all but ninety-two hereditary peers have been excluded.

The Lords was never politically representative, the great majority being Conservative supporters. Well, they would be, wouldn't they, when they owned those big houses and estates.

In 1997, a mere 12 per cent of peers represented Labour even though it had a massive Commons majority . About a third of the Upper House's members are known as cross-benchers, meaning they have no political affiliation, not that they dress in a strange way, though they do.

The Lords and Commons share many functions, especially in scrutinising the government. However, the Lords is much weaker and its powers have diminished considerably. Peers tend to focus on the detail of legislation rather than its principle and won't overturn something which appeared in the government's election manifesto.

At times they do arise and defeat the government, forcing ministers to think again. But the Commons has the power to tell the Lords to get stuffed and will pass a Bill anyway, even if the peers have been showing eminent sense. That shows them who the real boss is, doesn't it?

No, Minister

As that brilliantly insightful television series *Yes, Minister* made clear, it isn't really politicians who run the country. They only think they do.

The ones with their hands firmly on the levers of power are the civil servants, that massive unelected band who remain secure behind their desks in Whitehall whatever voters decide.

If you asked how many civil servants there are in Britain, most people would give the same answer: Too many. The precise number, at the last count, was 527,250, but it's difficult to be exact as the figure keeps creeping up remorselessly.

In 2004, Gordon Brown announced a vicious cull of Whitehall jobs. He was going to slash the number by 84,150. At that time there were 465,700 so, as anyone good at maths will instantly spot, instead of losing 84,150 civil servants, he managed to gain an extra 61,550 in Whitehall alone, with thousands more jumping on the bandwagon elsewhere. In the last three months of 2009 alone, another 23,000 joined the public sector. But that's the problem with the civil service – every opposition party and every prospective government sternly insists that it will make big cuts, yet instead the Men (and Women) in Whitehall keep on reproducing.

The number of civil servants is only a fraction of the workers paid by the state – i.e. us, the taxpayer. There are more than six million, including the armed forces, almost everyone in education and, greatest of all, the one and a quarter million who work in the National Health Service, the world's biggest employer after the Chinese army and Indian railways. It includes the huge numbers employed by local councils – the average county council has as many people working for it as the entire European Union (not something you ever hear from the anti-European brigade). Plus prison officers, judges and, of course, Members of Parliament. No wonder the public sector wage bill has reached £158 billion.

A couple of words of warning, though, before you start applauding politicians who swear they will slash these jobs. Firstly, you or someone in your family may well be among those six million and not too keen to be put out of work. Secondly, politicians give the impression that they can painlessly dump tens of thousands of bowler-hatted desk-bound non-productive bureaucrats. Certainly the civil service does harbour some of these but the majority of public employees are doing work that makes this a modern, civilised society. It's a difficult balancing act and more than one minister has toppled over while trying to keep it in equilibrium.

It's party time

In its early years, politics consisted of individuals doing their own thing, which meant forming alliances with other individuals over particular issues, from time to time, as the mood and necessity dictated. Eventually it became clear that these arrangements could be formalised – if the Duke of X was regularly getting together with Baron Y (in the nicest possible way) it made sense for them to have a permanent alliance. And so the party system was born.

Anyone can start a political party and anyone still does. The past few years have seen the creation of the Death, Dungeons and Taxes Party, the Mongolian Barbecue Great Place to Party Party and the Church of the Militant Elvis Party, not to mention the Miss Great Britain Party.

None of them has ever pretended that its members (if they have any) should go back to their constituencies and prepare for government, as one leader of the Liberal Democrats famously did. For, with the way the voting system currently works, discriminating against small parties, there are really only three that matter. Here is all you need to know about them.

Who's feeling blue?

The Conservative Party is very old and so are most of its members. Although they currently have a youthful leader and a shadow Cabinet that looks as if it is on work experience, the people who populate the constituency branches look back with affection to the time when Britain had an Empire, a period which seems like only yesterday to them.

History: Around 1680, when Charles II was on the throne, an alliance was formed by supporters of the Duke of York. This became the Tory Party and hundreds of years later its members are still content to be marched to the top of the hill and then marched down again without grumbling or complaining. For most of their existence, this has been the party of forelock-tuggers.

They were called the Tories after a group of Irish bandits yet waited until the 1830s to rebrand themselves as Conservatives, rather like Labour rechristened itself New Labour 160 years later. Despite the best efforts of those nineteenth-century marketing men, they have never shaken off being called Tories – or, for that matter, bandits, their opponents continuing to accuse them of robbing the poor to give to the rich.

From its inception, this has been the natural party of government. It has generally managed to select leaders with a genius for knowing which way the wind was blowing and bending with it. Ideology was not something that particularly concerned them. Power was more important than principle. Others could come up with revolutionary ideas but the voters were content to stick with the Tories, rather like preferring to wear an old coat because it is comfortable.

When voters did decide they wanted something different – like a wider franchise or a national health service – the Conservatives were quick to embrace it and move on to that territory.

And so it went on for almost 300 years until the whirling dervish that was Margaret Hilda Thatcher arrived. The grocer's daughter from Grantham was a revolutionary and not only because she was the first woman to become Prime Minister. Mrs Thatcher *believed* in things and, what's more, she attracted a doting following who believed in *her*. She was a twentieth-century Boudicca whose supporters would happily have painted themselves with woad (it is blue, after all) and run naked around Parliament Square if she had ordered them to.

Sadly for her, and them, the voters who had given her three general election victories eventually went off her in a big way. So the ruthless men in grey suits who ultimately call the shots dumped her because, when it came down to it, much as they idolised her, they loved power more.

Following her defenestration, civil war broke out in the Conservative Party. A succession of leaders each did worse than the one before. Until David Cameron arrived and got the Tories back on track. Sort of.

That's all you need to know about the Conservatives. They have had other leaders you might have heard of. Winston Churchill, the wartime Prime Minister who smoked cigars. Disraeli, who was Jewish and wrote books and was an unsung plumber (see section on Downing Street above). And, er, that's it.

Just remember, if you are ever fortunate enough to get invited for tea with the Tories, *do* mention Mrs Thatcher and *don't* mention Europe.

Seeing red

The Labour Party was born out of the trade union movement a century ago and pretty quickly became one of the two main parties, relegating the poor old Liberals to also-rans.

From the start it had a structural flaw. It represented the working man (and woman, sometimes) but most of the people who rose to the top were rather posher. A cynic might say that Labour's greatest achievement in the twentieth century was to keep the Tories in almost continuous power.

In their few periods in charge they did manage some notable things. Like founding the National Health Service. Most of all, though, they fought each other with a fury and passion that would sensibly have been reserved for their political enemies. In particular, the Labour Party has always hated its leaders. They are viewed as traitors who have sold principle down the river. They are never left-wing enough (except Michael Foot, who was ineluctably unelectable). Success at the ballot box was never enough.

Though there is a caveat. The unions which created the party and continue to largely fund it want Labour in power. Not only is this to the advantage of their members, in theory, though often not in practice, but it allows the union bosses access to Downing Street. At one time they were regularly invited in for beer and sandwiches over the Cabinet table but when Tony Blair arrived he preferred inviting pop stars and billionaire City traders to quaff Chablis and snack on canapés.

Until Blair, Labour struggled to win and retain power. Harold Wilson won four elections but three were with bare majorities. It was only with the creation of New Labour, a marketing man's dream led by Britain's greatest salesman, Tony Blair, that the party at last stood atop the political pinnacle.

But fratricide is never more than a dagger-stab away in the Labour Party. Gordon Brown and his henchmen spent ten years briefing against Blair and his supporters, knifing them in the back, front, side and every other part, until none were left and he rose from the bloodied field of battle to ascend the throne, trailing entrails and gore behind him.

It was ever thus in the Labour Party, just as it was for much of the history of the British monarchy. But though the monarchy has moved on to more civilised ways of behaviour, it is unlikely that the Labour Party ever will.

Clear yellow water

Once upon a time there was the Liberal Party and a great party it was. But when Labour arrived on the scene, it offered an alternative to which traditional Liberal supporters drifted.

You know what it's like when you have a party and no one comes. Well, that's what happened to the Liberals. Come election time, they were faced with the political equivalent of standing around pensively with stacks of stale French bread, hardening cheese and unopened cheap wine.

At the 1906 election they had 399 MPs. By 1924 they were down to forty and just eleven at the post-war poll. At one time they only had six MPs and the joke was that you could get the entire parliamentary Liberal Party in the back of a taxi.

When a new centrist party was formed in 1981 by a breakaway group from the wildly left-wing Labour Party of that era, it could have been the end of the Libs. Instead, it was the start of a resurgence. In fact the alliance formed between the Liberals and the fledgling Social Democratic Party was so successful that it led to one of their leaders, David Steel, telling conference delegates to 'go back to your constituencies and prepare for government.' If he had been more realistic, he should have told them to go back and prepare for another Tory landslide.

The result of that debacle was a merger between the Liberals and SDP to form the inventively named Liberal Democrats. They remain very much the third party although they did get sixty-two MPs elected in 2005. Whenever there is talk of a hung Parliament, there is much flirting with and courting of Lib Dem leaders.

But the more usual attitude of other parties to the Liberal Democrats is one of contempt because their members commit the unpardonable sin in today's political world of being interested in politics. Fringe meetings at their conference can go on for hours as delegates debate extraordinarily dull and incomprehensible subjects with fervour. Anyone thinking of attending would be well advised to take sandwiches and a thermos of tea – even if you don't need them, they will help you fit in.

As a party, the Lib Dems resemble one of those oddball characters you see in the street saying 'I told you the world would end today'. It is true that they have been right on a number of issues but no one listened to them then and they don't now.

As well as their parliamentary successes, they control a disproportionate number of local councils. This they do through their chameleon approach to elections. They are left-wing in inner cities where Labour is the main opposition, right-wing in the shires where they are taking on the Tories. Their leadership is the most pro-European of any party yet their voters are the most sceptical.

And now for something a bit different

The weakening of the two-party state of Labour and Conservative has not only resulted in a spurt for the Liberal Democrats. Voters disenchanted with the main parties have found other alternatives.

That is particularly true in Scotland and Wales, where the nationalist duo, the Scottish National Party and Plaid Cymru, have seen a terrific boost in their electoral support. The SNP has even become the largest party in the Scottish Parliament, and runs a minority administration (the other parties sulkily refuse to serve in a coalition with them). Plaid is the junior partner (with Labour) in the Welsh Assembly's administration.

The SNP has seven seats in the Westminster Parliament and Plaid has three, though those numbers belie their growing roles as the main challengers to Labour in Scotland and Wales.

The Green Party is providing an alternative, not just for fringe voters who believe the environment is the most important issue facing the country (still a small minority, despite green issues being pushed up everyone's agenda), but attracting serious support from voters generally disenchanted with the big three. Its highlights have been securing 15 per cent of the vote in the 1989 European election and getting two seats in the European Parliament in 2009.

Yet still, because of the unfairness of the UK electoral system, the Greens have never managed to get an MP elected.

Despite the strength of the party system, in theory it is possible for anyone to stand as an independent and be triumphantly voted into Parliament. But until the 1997 general election, there hadn't been an independent MP for almost half a century.

Then white-suited BBC reporter Martin Bell stood on an anti-sleaze ticket and swept to victory. He was followed at the next election by a retired doctor, Richard Taylor, whose campaign was entirely based around a campaign to keep his local hospital open.

In his acceptance speech, Dr Taylor spoke for unhappy voters all over the country when he said: 'I view this as a tremendous reaction from the people against powerful government and a very powerful political system that overrides the will of the people.'

As they say at Westminster: Hear, hear!

The fringe and beyond

As well as the sort of bonkers tiny parties already mentioned, there are a few which are very much of the fringe but have pretensions that belie their size. Rather like a poorly endowed bloke who thinks he is the office stud. Their grand ambition is not just to be taken seriously but to break into the mainstream and become one of the main parties. This is known to psychiatrists as delusions of grandeur and to the big parties as a real worry.

The most successful fringe party at the moment is the United Kingdom Independence Party, usually known as UKIP (as in 'You kip if you want to, I'm going to stay awake through this very long speech about the dangers of the European Union and why we would be better off if we were Iceland.') The best thing you can say about its leaders is that they don't believe in world domination. On the contrary, they don't want anything to do with the world. Their ambition is for the UK to remain forever a small island floating blissfully off the coast of the USA.

Another fringe party currently on the rise is the British National Party. It continues to attract support, mainly from sections of the white working class, by a) insisting it is not a racist party; and b) insisting even more passionately that there is no place for anyone in this country who isn't white. No doubt buoyed by his appearance on the BBC's *Question Time*, their leader Nick Griffin believes the BNP could become a big party. He may be encouraged in that thought by his study of history at Cambridge when he learnt how the German National Socialist Party was nowhere in the 1920s and considered a joke – yet within a decade, look where they and their leader were.

The best known genuinely fringe party remains the Monster Raving Loony Party, founded by the rock singer Screaming Lord Sutch, whose motto was 'There is nothing more monstrous than politicians'. Now there was a man before his time. When he was alive, Lord Sutch could be relied on to fight every by-election and the most frightening thing about him wasn't that he attracted a respectable number of votes (for a Raving Loony) but that some of the things he said made more sense than the utterings of the 'sensible' candidates.

It remains a source of wonder that completely crazy parties – ones that make the Monster Raving Loonies look respectable – actually attract supporters. For instance, the Mongolian Barbecue etc. Party mentioned above stood in Wimbledon in 1997 and attracted 112 votes. Isn't that incredible? To think that there are 112 people in Wimbledon who could be bothered to turn out on a politically historic day and cast their votes for the Mongolian thingummy candidate. They can't all have been Wombles.

It's war

If you have got this far and still think there are no good reasons for not voting, let us consider what should be the clincher. Of all the things a government can do, the most serious is going to war. That's so obvious it shouldn't need saying. War involves people dying. Hundreds of them, sometimes thousands. Often with appalling consequences for years or decades.

When we talk about 'The war' we usually mean the 1939–45 war to stop Hitler. But there have been a lot more since then. Korea, Suez, the Falklands, Gulf War I, Afghanistan and, of course, Gulf

War II, more commonly known as the invasion of Iraq. Although in 1939 the Prime Minister, Neville Chamberlain, went on the wireless to announce to the British people that 'this country is at war with Germany', none of the more recent hostilities has been accompanied by a declaration that they had commenced.

The retaking of the Falkland Islands after they had been seized by Argentina was actually called the Falklands *Conflict*, as if the British people could be fooled about the purpose of sending a huge armada halfway round the world. But at least there was a passionate debate in Parliament before the fleet was despatched.

When Tony Blair ordered British forces into Iraq to depose Saddam Hussein, he got the backing of Parliament on the basis of a lot of misinformation in a dodgy dossier. How can this be? How is it that MPs are allowed to argue and vote on the most trivial aspects of government policy yet our forces can be sent to fight and die on the whim of the Prime Minister?

The answer is that, in theory, the power to make war resides with the monarch but is actually exercised by the Prime Minister when his ministers are supine and cowed as they are today.

In the US, the President is the commander-in-chief of the armed forces but our Prime Ministers aren't, though some like to think they are. Mrs Thatcher enjoyed nothing better than donning a headscarf (so her hair didn't get mussed up) and clambering into a tank. She would have been at home in the SAS. By contrast, Gordon Brown wears a suit and tie when visiting our troops in the desert. You can't imagine him in battle fatigues.

The trouble with Prime Ministers playing war games is that real people die. Hundreds of British forces in Iraq and Afghanistan and untold thousands of civilians from those countries. Perversely, it was better when we had the nuclear threat. Prime ministers could puff themselves up with the self-importance of knowing they could press the red button (that now being confined to choosing what to watch on Sky) and blow the world into smithereens but none were mad enough to do it.

With the end of the Cold War, even the most hawkish Pentagon chief doesn't really believe there is much of a threat of nuclear war, even if some crazed terrorist does get his hands on a DIY make-your-own-atomic-bomb kit. However, that hasn't stopped our government insisting that we must go on building, buying and investing in nuclear weapons. Without a vote.

They are the ultimate political phallic symbol. Not for nothing are atomic missiles shaped like a penis. The major myth around nukes is that there can be a British independent nuclear deterrent. That the UK can stand completely alone and fire off one or more without reference to any of our allies, especially the USA.

Can you imagine the scene?

The hotline rings in 10 Downing Street.

PRIME MINISTER: Hallo?
PRESIDENT: Hi. Is there something you'd like to tell me?
PM: Er, about what?
PRESIDENT: Have you been a naughty boy?
PM *(laughing nervously)*: I jolly well hope not.
PRESIDENT: Have you been pressing any buttons lately? Firing off anything into the air?
PM: Oh, that. Yes, well, I suppose I have.
PRESIDENT: That was very silly, wasn't it?

But there is no reply as the Prime Minister, Downing Street, Westminster, London, England, the rest of the UK and most of western Europe have just disappeared under a mushroom cloud as whoever was targeted retaliated.

No, an independent nuclear deterrent was just a daft big boys' conceit. Yet billions and billions of pounds of our money has been spent on the pretence.

Now do you still think voting changes anything?

How you decide to vote is very much a personal choice. Here nuns pray for divine guidance before casting theirs. (Joe Dunne/Hulton Archive/Getty Images)

The politics industry

Of all the growth industries in the past century, politics takes pride of place. There is a good reason why motoring, flying, TV and computers have blossomed (i.e., they didn't exist a century ago) but politics had been around for hundreds of years when the twentieth century dawned, albeit usually in an amateur form. Yet there has been an extraordinary explosion in the number of people involved, what they do and the impact they have on our lives.

In 1900 there were sixty government ministers: nineteen in the Cabinet, ten outside and thirty-one junior ministers. Thirty-three of the sixty posts were held by MPs and the remaining twenty-seven by peers – in fact, eight of the nineteen Cabinet ministers were aristocrats. Seven had gone to Eton and fourteen to Oxford or Cambridge.

Today there are some 130 people in the government and the Cabinet has twenty-two members, only three of them in the Lords, including the Leader of that House.

But that is nothing compared with the incredible increase in the number of people employed in the public sector since 1900. In fact, there were so few then, statistics don't seem to have been kept of how many there were.

While considering that explosion in state employment, remember that at the start of the twentieth century the UK was responsible for governing the British Empire, which covered 11 million square miles and had a population exceeding 450 million. Today it doesn't. So what are all those extra ministers (not to mention civil servants) doing?

Spinning in democracy's grave

No area of politics has experienced a greater growth in activities and personnel than the spin industry. It has come from nowhere to dominate the political scene. Before the 1970s there were hardly any press officers yet now there are battalions of manipulators dedicated to fooling the public and puffing up the government or local council which employs them and to whom they are more dedicated than Greyfriars Bobby was to his dead master.

The original press officers naively considered that their job was answering questions posed by journalists (most of them were former journalists themselves, so they not only knew the needs of that trade but nurtured the desire to get back to the 'proper job' they used to do). Today's spin doctors are not interested in what the media wants to know – or the public, for that matter. Their only concern is serving their political masters, rather like cardinals in the medieval Roman

Catholic Church. The media hates spin doctors while relying on them and obsequiously fawning on them. The public doesn't completely grasp their sheer cynicism and anti-democratic nature, thinking that the insight given by *The Thick of It* couldn't possibly be accurate (It is. Painfully accurate). Even politicians attack them from time to time. Yet no party leader dares not have a spin doctor of his own.

The most vilified of the sordid bunch remains Alastair Campbell, who was Tony Blair's Rottweiller and the second most important person in the government (some, including Campbell, would say *the* most important). He wasn't the first spin doctor, though, and he certainly isn't the last. Gordon Brown has employed a series of brutes, including one who had to go after being discovered making up and disseminating vile stories not just about Tories but Labour MPs not totally supportive of their master.

Now the Conservatives have a leader who was once a junior spin doctor himself and employs a former editor of the *News of the World* as his mouthpiece.

The Bible was wrong about the meek. It is the brash who have inherited the earth.

It is commonly thought that what spin doctors do is tell lies on behalf of their masters. Their job is much more complicated than that. In the world they exist in, everything their boss does is good, he has never made a mistake, even when it is obvious to everyone in the country that he has committed some appalling act of folly, so will never, but never, apologise, as that is an admission of fault. By contrast, everything their opponents do is wrong, bad and criminally irresponsible. The conjugation of the verb 'to spin' is:

I am perfect
You are useless
He is a complete tosser
She is the wife of a complete tosser.

The third leg of the spin doctor's art is to manipulate the media by granting favours to a chosen few, a magic circle of sycophants and patsies, while monstering those who dare to write a word out of place. Stories are given to journalists who are sympathetic while those who are not are starved of 'exclusives', thus lining them up for bollockings from their editors for not getting stories. Top spin doctors ring up journalists and editors and sweet-talk them when they feel like it, but ring up and rant at them if they feel the line is not being toed. Which is often.

The black art of the spin doctor has so debased politics that it makes the expenses scandal look no worse than a wart on the body politic, yet most voters know little about this insidious operation. And, most insulting of all, spin doctors (particularly Alastair Campbell) blame journalists for lowering politics and politicians in the eyes of the public. That is because there are journalists who tell the truth about the way politicians behave – so whose fault is it if that makes them look like the equivalent of human snakes?

(Don't) read all about it

Which brings us seamlessly to the press and the question: What is the difference between the way newspapers cover politics and how they report football? The answer is that they have to be unbiased when they write about soccer.

Just imagine the furore there would be if a paper blatantly came out in support of Manchester United rather than City, or Arsenal over Tottenham, or Everton instead of Liverpool. Boycotts would be organised, bundles of newspapers would be burnt in the streets and reporters from that publication could find themselves banned from the ground.

But in politics, editors can be as partisan, biased and prejudiced as they like and it is considered to be part of the game. It is even enshrined in the Press Complaints Commission's code of practice. The *Telegraph*, *Mail* and *Express* are devotedly behind the Conservatives to varying degrees of slavishness while the *Mirror* does the same for Labour. The *Sun* worshipped at Mrs Thatcher's hem when she was Prime Minister, hated John Major, switched to support Tony Blair and has now gone back to the Tories. The *Guardian* leans to the left. So does the *Independent*, though it advised its readers to vote Conservative for the first years of its life.

Does anyone take any notice, though? Well, yes they do. The public don't – even the diminishing band who still read newspapers – but politicians and journalists are obsessed with what the papers are saying. When the *Sun* said it was switching from Conservative to Labour, the 'story' led all the news broadcasts, as it did when the paper changed back to the Tories.

Politicians who insist they don't read the papers are liars. They are fixated on them. A word of praise can send a warm glow through the most hard-bitten minister while mild criticism can spark a fury that lays low all who have the misfortune to cross his path.

While it's clearly not pleasant to have rude things written about you, the idea that newspapers have the power to swing tens of thousands of votes and so win elections for their chosen party is a delusion of grandeur held only by proprietors, editors and politicians. It's actually an insult to the intelligence of the electorate.

Can they seriously believe that anyone picks up a paper, reads something urging them to vote one way and says 'Gosh, I was going to vote for the other lot, but I'm not now'? Besides, if readers voted as their newspaper told them to, there would never have been a Labour government before 1997, the great bulk of papers having supported the Tories before then.

The other common fallacy is that political journalists on the

whole loathe politicians. They may write as if they don't but the
truth is that they need each other like a drunk needs another drink.

In fact, drinking is an important part of their relationship, as
is eating. Hacks and politicians drink together in the nineteen bars
in the Palace of Westminster and dine together on the journalists'
generous expenses. Most insidiously, they share secrets through the
infamous 'lobby system'.

This is how it works (and if you believe in the freedom of the
press, look away now). A politician tells a journalist something 'on
a lobby basis'. This means he can write the story but not say who
told him. So the story will say something like 'The government
is planning to invade Greece in retaliation for their demand to
return the Elgin marbles, according to a Foreign Office source'.
Or 'The opposition is drawing up plans to scrap the state pension
and give the money to Eton, Harrow and other public schools, a
Whitehall insider has revealed'.

Politicians claim that ridiculous stories such as these, which appear
almost daily in one paper or another, are made up by journalists. They
rarely are. Journalists don't have that much imagination. They are
made up by politicians to discredit other politicians or boost their
own side or test some ridiculous plan which wouldn't see the light of
day in a thousand years. Yet journalists publish them because they are
terrified that, if they don't, another paper will.

In the real world, you might think an editor would be delighted
if a rival ran a ludicrous story about plans to invade Greece or
abolish the old-age pension. In Media Gulch, however, editors
go ballistic and demand to know why their staff failed to get this
exclusive (the answer 'Because it is an invented load of total tosh'
is not acceptable). And that is what passes for political reporting in
Great Britain today.

Addendum: These fantasy stories are regularly picked up by the
columnists who infest British newspapers like streptococci and are

commented on furiously as if they are not just true but an outrage to
the British people. As this is the principal way in which information
is disseminated in this country, is it any wonder so many voters have
such a bizarre view of the world?

An impossible balancing act

In contrast to newspapers, broadcasters are supposed to treat all
political parties equally, so a whole load of rules about balance and
fairness are imposed on them which don't apply to the press – or,
when it comes down to it, to life.

At the BBC, which has the strictest rules of all, there are Very
Important People whose job is simply to make sure it can never,
ever be accused of bias. Does this mean it never is? Of course
not. All parties complain all the time. The Tories say it is biased
against them, Labour insists it is biased against the government and
the Liberal Democrats are convinced they don't get a big enough
crack of the whip. Small parties moan that they never get a look
in, however many look-ins they have. The BNP gets cross that they
aren't on air enough while the other parties think it outrageous that
the BNP are on air at all.

Broadcasting bigwigs used to complacently claim that if
everyone was complaining, they must have got it about right.
That is not possible in the age of the spin doctor. The political
parties employ teams of alert young activists to monitor everything
that goes out and shoot off complaints, corrections, insults and,
occasionally, praise (just to destabilise the broadcasters who can't
decide if the spin doctors mean it or are being sarcastic).

It is so childish it is like a gaggle of three-year-olds
squabbling over who got the biggest scoop of ice cream. Come
election time, producers have to tot up the number of minutes
and seconds that were devoted to Labour and make sure it is

the same for the Conservatives and Lib Dems. Which is why the Scottish National Party (who do govern Scotland, after all) demanded the right to be part of the TV election debates.

It is also why during elections newsreaders say at the end of a report about a particular constituency: 'There are thirty-nine other people standing in this election . . . a full list can be found on our website.' Thank God for the internet. TV used to have to scroll a list of all the candidates across the screen.

In other countries, broadcasters can be as partisan as they like. In America, for example, Fox television is so right-wing it makes George W. Bush look like a woolly liberal. Yet in this country, Rupert Murdoch's News Corporation, which owns Fox, runs Sky, which maintains exemplary balance between the parties – some would say it is better at it than the BBC.

Without advocating the Fox way, a growing number of people think the broadcasting rules should be relaxed and the public treated like adults. Why should there be such different standards for TV and radio from newspapers – and blogs?

For your elucidation, this is a very brief excerpt from the BBC's Producer Guidelines on principles of political impartiality:

- *We must treat matters of public policy or political or industrial controversy with due accuracy and impartiality in our news services and other output.*
- *We must not express an opinion on current affairs or matters of public policy other than broadcasting.*
- *We must not campaign, or allow ourselves to be used to campaign.*

The whole document is 200 pages long so the BBC bureaucracy clearly spent a huge amount of time, effort and man-hours producing it rather than concentrating on making programmes. Perhaps they will one day make a Jane Austen-type 24-part costume drama of it. The opening line could be: 'It is a truth universally acknowledged that a broadcasting organisation in possession of a good fortune must be in want of producer guidelines.'

Lights, camera, no action

By the end of the 1980s, television had invaded just about every aspect of our way of life. Except one. The House of Commons, the great bosom of democracy, was modestly kept away from the prying eye of TV cameras.

Given that the first television outside broadcast was in 1937 for the coronation of King George VI while twenty-seven million viewers marvelled at the Queen being crowned in black and white in 1953, it's staggering that Parliament was so slow to join the TV age. The authorities must have thought it wouldn't catch on.

It wasn't until 1978, more than fifty years after the BBC was founded, that there was even radio coverage of Westminster and a wider audience for the first time heard the words 'Order! Order!' in the distinctive Welsh lilt of the then Speaker, George Thomas.

Back in 1964 the government had recommended a trial period of letting the cameras in. Proposal rejected, although there was a three-day experiment in the House of Lords four years later. And a mere seventeen years after that, peers actually let television record their proceedings.

The reason MPs resisted televising the Commons for so long was that they thought it would encourage exhibitionism. That was like worrying that car ownership would encourage driving. The Commons, and politics generally, exists to satisfy the lust for exhibitionism of a section of the population. MPs show off – that is what they do for a living.

What the powers-that-be were really worried about was that TV cameras would inevitably change their behaviour – including dissuading members of the front benches from lolling around with their feet up on the table between them or arriving to vote at 10 p.m. in evening dress.

It has to be said that televising Parliament did affect how some MPs dressed. Who would have thought before that magic day in November 1989 when the cameras first rolled that soon women MPs would be sporting bright pink suits, shoulder pads and artfully draped scarves? Perhaps TV should have stayed away on the grounds of taste.

When the Commons finally agreed to being televised, a compromise was reached by the imposition of very strict rules governing what could be shown. Television is not allowed to film close-ups or the reactions of MPs, which makes for pretty dull viewing. When protestors threw purple powder at the Prime Minister in the House, he could be shown ducking and brushing it off, but the throwers had to remain off camera.

The tight rules explain the habit of 'doughnutting', when those who want to be on telly make sure they sit close to someone who is going to make an important speech. It is also a device that makes it appear to the viewer that the chamber is packed because the person speaking is surrounded on all sides by other members in an otherwise empty chamber. However, broadcasters have gradually relaxed the rules, which is why when the cameras show the whole House, you can see there are only six MPs on the government benches – one speaking and five clustered around him as if they are huddling together for warmth.

So one thing the cameras did do – and what those opposed to TV feared – was to show how few members are present for many important debates. They also revealed how white, middle-aged and male the House of Commons was and the public-school raucousness after members have had a good lunch.

On the positive side, television has been there to record moments of history, such as Tory deputy leader Geoffrey Howe sticking the verbal knife into Margaret Thatcher and former Foreign Secretary Robin Cook's principled resignation over the Iraq invasion, as well as the dignity of Parliament on occasions like the deaths of Labour leader John Smith and David Cameron's young son Ivan.

Up the polls

Like spin doctoring, opinion polls have been one of modern politics' great growth areas. The media as well as politicians are obsessed with them, though politicos play a silly game of saying they never take any notice of polls. Really?

Polls work like this. A polling company employs researchers who call up people at random (they used to stop them in the street) and ask which way they would vote if there were an election tomorrow. If it is a long time before the next election, this is a silly and irrelevant question, like asking someone which member of their family they would eat first if they were stranded on a desert island.

The traditional method of polling is now being replaced by respondents replying to questions on the internet. That seems even less scientific.

Yet opinion polls on the whole have been proved to be remarkably accurate in revealing voting trends and in the actual result of elections as election day approaches.

They certainly give the newspapers that commission them good exclusive stories, particularly if the poll happens to be wrong. This is how that bit of nonsense operates. Let's say there are half-a-dozen political polls a month and five of them, in common with the six from the previous month and the six from the month before, show that the Tories have a lead of around 12 points. Then one poll comes up with a Conservative lead of just 8 points. Sensation! Tories slump in popularity! Labour closes the gap dramatically! Are the Tories on the skids? Could Labour sneak up and actually win the election? These are the questions on which thousands of words are expended.

The answer can be given in one word, though: No. Or at least it is on the evidence of this poll. The near certainty is that this is a rogue survey, as will be revealed when the next ones come out showing the Conservatives with a lead of, yes, you've got it, around 12 points. But that truth hasn't prevented not just the paper that commissioned the rogue poll but all the others and the broadcasters merrily, sensationally and learnedly banging on about something that is plainly wrong.

We will deal with polling during election campaigns later but this taste of the science of gauging public opinion should have shown that there is more wrong with the journalists who interpret them and the politicians who slavishly believe them than there is with the much-criticised pollsters.

A little local difficulty

Of course, people aren't only represented by Members of Parliament. There are councillors, too, on their local councils – and a fine array of those there are. County councils, district councils and parish councils in addition to unitary and metropolitan authorities. These are at times treated with contempt by Westminster politicians (except when they want them to work at election time) but they are usually closer to the voters and are responsible for some of the main services enjoyed by the population (like schools and refuse collection), as well as some of the horrors that blight their lives (such as traffic wardens and council tax).

Local councils are responsible for most of the day-to-day stuff in our lives. They run care homes, the police, fire fighters, education, libraries, street cleaning, planning and bus services. They look after

96 per cent of the country's roads, spend £12 billion a year on housing and employ around three million people.

Yet the turnout in local elections is considerably lower than in parliamentary elections – in some places, just half the figure, with one in three of those eligible to vote bothering to do so.

Teetering on the borders

Scotland became part of the United Kingdom in 1707 but, as every Scot will tell you, it never lost its identity or the wish to have more control over its affairs than Westminster allowed. The procession of Scots travelling south to run the UK did not diminish this desire.

In 1999, almost 300 years after being subsumed under the rulers of the rest of these islands, Scotland got its own parliament back.

At the same time, Wales, which had been roped in with England constitutionally since 1536, was given its own assembly. Not parliament, please note, just an assembly.

These concessions to the Scots and Welsh were supposed to end the demand by a minority of their populations for independence. It did no such thing. And it has started a hare running which may be difficult to put back in the bottle, if that isn't too mixed a metaphor.

The people of Scotland and Wales now have the opportunity to vote for their representatives in these new bodies (as well as still having MPs at Westminster, to the annoyance of some English politicians). Watch this space.

Continental drift

Few things arouse such passion or extraordinary emotions as the subject of Europe or, to be specific, the European Union. Europe itself is OK. It means sunshine holidays by the Mediterranean, delicious food and cheap booze. But the European Union! That stands for the jackboots of our old enemies across the Channel taking over this country by underhand devices because they could not defeat us militarily.

In fact, the EU is the most remarkable and successful grouping of independent sovereign nations the world has ever seen. It also has a parliament which we can vote for (or, at least, for the British members).

Considering what a red-hot issue Europe is supposed to be – it brought down a Conservative government and nearly destroyed the party, and now has spawned the United Kingdom Independence Party – not many people in this country can be bothered to turn out and vote for their MEPs once every five years; only one in three at the last EU election, just about the lowest of the twenty-seven member states.

Yet anti-Europeans keep banging on about 80 per cent (give or take a few distorted percentage points) of our laws being made in Brussels. (This is not true. Independent analyses suggest the figure is somewhere around 12 to 15 per cent). So if the EU is so central to the way this country is run and if the British people are so incensed by it, why don't they turn up and vote in the elections for its parliament? Even if it was for the Monster Raving European Loony Party.

Despotism of the masses

No mention of Europe is complete nowadays without dealing with referendums because of the fuss made about the Lisbon Treaty. But what are they? Simply a different way of voting – instead of choosing someone to be your MP or other representative, you vote Yes or No on a particular topic.

Other countries and some American states have them regularly. Britain does not. In fact there has only ever been one, in 1975, and that was on whether the UK should remain in the Common Market, although referendums have been held in Scotland and Wales on devolution.

The reason people want and don't want referendums is very simple. You want one because you know you are going to win and you don't want one because you know you are going to lose.

Referendums have a nasty habit of going a particular way because people don't vote on the question they are asked but on how much they loathe the government of the day. Which is usually a lot. So they vote No because they hate the government, not because they don't want to support whatever it is they are being asked to decide. It's stupid, but that's democracy. Or is it?

There is no tradition of referendums in this country because, far from being democratic in expressing the will of the people (which may change from day to day anyway) they represent a kind of anarchy. They are despotism by the baser instincts of the population rather than of principles. In other countries, they have been used by dictators of right and left to create the myth that they are in touch with the people they rule with an iron fist.

Our way of doing things is to elect representatives who then act on our behalf. Referendums are decidedly not British yet, ironically, they are being demanded as a tool to prevent our way of life being overrun by European ways of doing things.

The dirty bits

There have been call girls, rent boys, mistresses, love children, dodgy business deals, 'cash for honours', questionable home loans and outright corruption throughout the history of Parliament. No worse, no better than anywhere several hundred people are stuck together, working silly hours, away from normal life and often being treated as though they are special and can therefore get away with being naughty.

What has changed over the years is that we have found out about it. Previously the press was too polite and deferential to dream of publishing details of scandals involving the ruling classes, even though insiders knew what was going on. That attitude has long since vanished, which is either a good or bad thing depending on whether you're an MP with a cupboard full of skeletons or a journalist.

Disraeli (Tory) was notoriously bad with money and borrowed the equivalent of £4 million to buy himself a country home, which has echoes of the scandal that led to the first resignation of Peter Mandelson (Labour). Except Dizzy never paid back his loan.

Lloyd George (Liberal) openly had a mistress and sold peerages to raise money for his party. Anthony Eden (Tory) was addicted to amphetamines, Harold Wilson (Labour) became entangled with crooks and Cecil Parkinson (Tory) had a long affair with his secretary and made her pregnant. He had to resign, but Paddy Ashdown (Liberal Democrat) saw his ratings go up when he admitted having a fling with his secretary. David Mellor (Tory) was caught out over a young actress who claimed he wore a Chelsea football shirt when he scored.

The most sensational political scandal involved John Profumo, the minister for war in Harold Macmillan's Conservative government. In the early 1960s he was having an affair with a young 'model' called Christine Keeler. This story had everything: high society (the relationship started at Cliveden, the country mansion owned by Lord Astor); intrigue, in that Keeler was also bonking a spy from the Russian embassy; tragedy, with the suicide of the society osteopath Stephen Ward after he was prosecuted for living off immoral earnings (i.e. introducing rich men to poor girls). But what finally did for Profumo was that he lied to the Commons. When rumours first surfaced, he was challenged in the House and denied everything. So when the truth emerged, he had to go. Making it plain to MPs that you can lie to your constituents, lie in the papers and on television – lie, in fact, wherever you like, as long as you don't lie in the Commons chamber.

The scandal which came closest to rivalling Profumo was the

prosecution of Jeremy Thorpe, the leader of the Liberal Party, over the killing of a great Dane belonging to a male model called Norman Scott, who was walking the dog when a hitman shot her. The incredible plot, according to the prosecution, was that Thorpe had wanted to warn off Scott (or possibly kill him, though you would have thought it was easy to spot the difference between a male model and a great Dane) because the Liberal leader had been having an affair with him and had been threatened with blackmail at a time when homosexuality was still illegal. In court, Scott described in painful detail how he was first seduced by Thorpe. Thorpe was acquitted but it was the end of his career.

If by now you are getting the impression that some Members of Parliament lead incredibly exotic lives, you wouldn't be wrong. And the list goes on. Labour MP John Stonehouse disappeared from a Miami beach in 1974, leaving behind his clothes. It was assumed this high-flying minister had drowned – until he turned up alive and well in Australia six months later living with his secretary and having set up a string of dodgy companies.

Jeffrey Archer, the Tory Party's pin-up boy, was jailed for perjury after lying in court about accusations that he'd had sex with a prostitute. Another glamorous Conservative, Jonathan Aitken, also went to prison for lying in court about staying at the Paris Ritz as guest of a Saudi Arabian businessman which, as Aitken was a government minister at the time, would have been a serious breach of parliamentary protocol. Labour's Ron Davies, the Secretary of State for Wales, will be remembered not for his contribution to the valleys but his wanderings on Clapham Common in south London. In what he called his 'moment of madness' he was mugged at knifepoint after inviting a total stranger he'd met on the Common to join him for supper. They had bumped into each other at a known meeting point for homosexuals though Davies claimed he had gone there to watch badgers.

The most concentrated eruption of parliamentary scandals came during the dying years of John Major's government. Not only did these include the money given by disgruntled Harrods owner Mohamed Al Fayed in brown envelopes to Tory MP Neil Hamilton to get him to ask questions in the Commons, but a backbench Conservative who was filmed virtually *in flagrante* on a park bench with an eighteen-year-old model (how these models have impacted on parliamentary life) when he was supposed to be out canvassing during the election.

Here is the photo used by Guy Fawkes on the parliamentary pass that allowed him to gain access in his attempt to blow the place up. For the first, but not the last, time, Commons authorities failed to spot that all was not as it should be – in this case, photography wasn't invented for another 250 years. (David Hattersley)

Life, death and really important things

The legendary Liverpool manager Bill Shankly once said that football wasn't a matter of life or death – it was more important than that. Some people feel the same about elections. Winning is everything.

They will sit for hours in freezing halls listening to the human equivalent of boiled cabbage bubbling on and on and on about something which seems to them more vital than turning up at their granny's funeral but less important than the result of the local under-eights Sunday morning kick-around to anyone else.

They will turn out in all weathers to knock on doors to ask people who clearly have no interest in anything if they are interested in joining the party. Or helping the party. Or just voting for it.

Elections are the time when these fanatics really come into their own. They are like junkies only allowed a fix once every five years and then indulging in an orgy. The anticipation is gripping. Will it be in March? Or May? Or June? And why? And what are the implications for each date?

They obsess about who will win. And what the margin will be. And what will happen after the election. They are told not to gloat and not to panic but that is like telling a starving man not to eat. They cannot get enough of newspaper articles or television commentating or debating and agonising with their equally obsessed friends.

And those are just the foot soldiers. It is impossible to over-state the hysteria of the parties' high commands, who are doing the equivalent of thrashing themselves with birch twigs in their frenzy. Everything, but everything, has to be planned in today's electioneering. Not just functions such as ordering leaflets and posters or making party political broadcasts but planning so meticulous that it covers the most irrelevant minutiae *just in case*. Nothing can be left to chance.

You don't get a sense of what happens from political text books. They say bland things like: 'An election is called when the Prime Minister requests the Queen to dissolve Parliament by Royal Proclamation.' If you think that is all there is to elections, you probably consider that having sex is no different from reading a manual describing how to do it.

During the period of an election campaign, the junkie does not sleep. He lives on whatever fast food is put in front of him (Tony Blair survived on bananas, Mrs Thatcher on eggs) and goes through so many highs and lows that a trip on the rollercoasters at Alton Towers would seem like a stroll across quiet countryside by comparison.

Elections weren't always like this. The most stimulating part of campaigns used to be public meetings, when candidates could be challenged by their constituents. But nationally it was all very low key. Clem Attlee, the Labour leader after the war, was driven around the country by his wife, getting out of his car from time to time to say to startled passers-by: 'Good morning. I am the leader of the Labour Party.' Today there is virtually no contact with members of the public – not since one of them threw an egg at John Prescott and his fist made contact with the member of the public.

Election campaigns are run so tightly that they make military campaigns look like amateur night at a holiday camp. Nothing, but nothing, is left to chance. Every word spoken, every photo taken, every policy announcement, every candidate paraded – all are vetted, inspected inside out and outside in, nursed and finally dribbled out for the elucidation of the electorate. Which is why the electorate learns practically nothing during an election campaign.

Size matters

To the outside observer, general election campaigns are about the leaders of the parties dashing around the country, making the odd speech, grinning a lot, shaking a ridiculous number of hands and doing the occasional interview. In fact, that is what it is about nowadays as far as the media and party leaders are concerned.

But strictly speaking the election should be about what happens in each individual constituency. None counts more than another, which is why your vote in Little Wittering or Blacktown East is as important as one cast by the electors in Kirkcaldy & Cowdenbeath for their MP, a certain Mr G. Brown, or in Witney for their member,

Mr D. Cameron. All constituencies are equal, though some are more equal than others.

It would be more democratic if they all had the same number of voters and were the same size but the world (and the UK) isn't like that. Some constituencies cover a huge area because they are in the country while others are quite small because they are in cities and their residents live in homes close together (think about it – how many isolated farmhouses hold the same number of people as one tower block?).

The principle is that every constituency has around 68,000 electors but the practice is different. The Isle of Wight, for example, has 110,000 voters. It could be made into two seats, with two MPs, but then each would only have 55,000 voters so it has been left as the nation's biggest electorate. It actually has five times more voters than the constituency with the smallest number, which is Na h-Eileanan an Iar on the west coast of Scotland. This couldn't be made into a bigger geographical area as it is already 130 miles from one end to the other.

This difference in size between constituencies is not just an interesting quirk, it is unfair. For it means it takes a lot more votes to elect your average Conservative MP, who tends to come from a rural area, than a Labour one, as they hold mainly urban seats. Most politicians, even Tories, keep quiet about this undemocratic gerrymandering as they believe it might make some people realise there is even more reason for not bothering to vote. It does mean, though, that those who live in large rural constituencies will have a wasted vote a) because a Tory will always be returned, even if the rest of the country goes over to Labour, as it did in 1997; and b) even if much of the rest of the country votes Conservative, the likelihood is you may still not get a Tory government because the odds are stacked against it.

Yet, bizarrely, people who live in those disadvantaged rural constituencies are actually quite good at going out to vote whereas in inner-city areas which would stick with Labour even if it was party policy to kill the first-born of all working-class families (a proposal narrowly rejected to replace Clause IV of the party's constitution), the turn-out is much lower.

A date with the Queen

The starting pistol is fired for the election race when the Prime Minister is driven down The Mall to Buckingham Palace where he asks the Queen to dissolve Parliament. He will have warned her he is coming, in case she is out shopping or getting her hair done, and Her Majesty, having gone through this rigmarole fourteen times already, will have a pretty good idea that he is not coming in to ask how the corgis are.

The election has to take place seventeen working days after that, which makes it about three and half weeks when weekends are taken into account. There is a widespread belief that elections are decided during this brief period but it is unlikely that the intense lobbying and propagandising that goes on has more than the most minimal effect on voters' intentions. The majority of people will have decided before it starts that they would rather cut off their head than vote for Party X or that they will stick with Party X come what may as they have supported it at every election since time began or maybe that on this occasion they will break the habit of a lifetime and give Party Y a chance, even if it means their grandfather will be turning in his grave. Or maybe that at this election they will simply stay at home.

Most effort goes into getting voters in marginal constituencies to turn out, for theirs are the votes that really matter. This used to happen by parties identifying their likely supporters and then badgering them on election evening if they hadn't been to the polling station. Today there are more sophisticated ways of getting to them but the idea is basically the same – identify them, get them out.

What appeals to political geeks about this form of electioneering is that you can see the effects of what you are doing. Other ways of fighting elections are less certain.

Channel Three

The modern equivalent of the candidates getting together in a draughty hall on a cold night is putting them head to head in a television studio so the nation can watch them debating the vital issues. Actually, it's not that modern. The Americans have been doing it for nearly half a century but, hey, we like to stick to our traditional ways. Besides, our usual way of dealing with televised election debates between party leaders is this: The leader of the opposition demands a debate. The Prime Minister rejects it. End of story.

This time it is different. There are going to be televised debates, three of them, between the three main party leaders. These are being hailed as the greatest breakthrough in British democracy since the invention of the ballot box. However, if they are anything like the weekly Prime Minister's Questions, voters will be none the wiser if they stay glued to every second of every debate.

There now follows. . .

. . .the sound of millions of people putting on the kettle, looking for the remote control or setting off to walk the dog. Yes, it's the announcer uttering the dreaded words 'There now follows a Party Political Broadcast on behalf of. . .'.

These are the closest you get to naked propaganda on our television and they exist because political parties are banned from advertising in this country. So, in a great British compromise, the parties are given these slots for free during election periods.

Politicians love them because they consider them to be the media equivalent of strapping down millions of voters so they can't escape and pumping into their brains the incontestable truth about how fantastic their party is and how useless their opponents are. Strangely, the viewers (those who can be bothered to keep watching) are rarely fooled.

The first PPB (as they are known in the trade, the letters uttered by television professionals with a curled lip) appeared on television during the 1951 election that returned Churchill to power. The great wartime leader was aged seventy-seven at the time, so the Liberals decided to use someone even older. Lord Samuel was eighty-one and about the least telegenic person imaginable. He appeared live, stumbled through the script – there were no teleprompters in those days – and over-ran his allotted time, so was cut off in mid-flow or, to be more accurate, mid-stumble.

This trend-setting broadcast did indeed set the trend for decades of barely intelligible broadcasts. Most of those from the 1950s featured men in suits talking directly into the camera, including a memorable Labour double act from Christopher Mayhew and Sir Hartley Shawcross. It began with Mayhew saying: 'You may be wondering how it happens that someone as well dressed, well educated and well off as Sir Hartley, how he comes to be in the Labour Party. What's your answer to that, Sir Hartley?' Now why can't John Humphrys or Jeremy Paxman come up with tough questions like that?

Of course, that is why politicians love party politicals. Those snarling journalists are kept out. On the rare occasions when one is allowed on to a PPB it is because he is a complete patsy. Alastair Campbell, then political editor of the *Daily Mirror*, quizzed Neil Kinnock on a PPB during the 1992 election campaign. The Labour leader was untroubled by any of his questions. Campbell, a personal friend of Kinnock, went on to prove his neutrality and journalistic integrity by becoming Tony Blair's spin doctor.

Long before then, politicians hit on the idea of making party political broadcasts mimic the TV shows of the day, as if they could fool the viewers into thinking they were watching a real programme. An early exponent of that art was Tony Benn, who appeared seated in a newscaster's swivel chair hosting a mock quiz show called *Political Challenge*.

The most dramatic innovation came in 1987, with the film which became known as *Kinnock: The Movie*. This was a biopic of the Labour leader produced by Hugh Hudson, the (Labour-supporting) Oscar-winning director of *Chariots of Fire*. The film did give him a 16 per cent lift in his personal ratings but, come election day, there was no Oscar for Mr Kinnock.

The Tories responded at the next election with *The Journey*, directed by (Tory-supporting) Oscar-winning director John Schlesinger, in which John Major feigned surprise at how little had changed when he returned to his childhood home in Brixton and met a lot of West Indians. Unfortunately none of the stall-holders and others he bumped into feigned surprise at being confronted by the Prime Minister.

And so to the big question: Do party political broadcasts really make any difference? They certainly cheer up their own side but it is unlikely that they change many minds.

It would be strange if they did. And the sort of mind that could be changed by a party political broadcast for one side could just as easily be swayed by one for the other side a few days later. There really is no point in them.

The greasy polls
The use of polls by the political and media classes has already been touched on but during election campaigns they achieve even greater

significance. No day goes by without at least one appearing. You might ask what their point is. Why should newspaper A want to dole out thousands of pounds for a poll when newspaper B did one yesterday, C the day before and D is doing one tomorrow? But they do, and each publication reads more into every one of them than Mystic Meg ever got out of a crystal ball.

The politicians' reaction to election polls is always the same. The party shown to be in the lead tries desperately not to look smug and says: 'There is only one poll that matters – the election.' The party that is behind tries desperately not to look suicidal and says: 'There is only one poll that matters – the election.'

On the whole, the polls are reasonably accurate, certainly over who is going to win, with their margin of error averaging out at 2 per cent. The election which caused real problems was the one in 1992, which produced the worst result in British polling history. Four out of five of the fifty polls carried out put Labour in the lead by as much as 7 per cent yet the Conservatives won 'the only poll that matters' by 9 per cent. After that debacle, the pollsters devised a better way to tell if people were lying to them about their voting intentions. No one has yet devised a way to tell if politicians are lying about their intentions.

Another kind of poll is carried out on the day of the election itself and is known as an exit poll because it involves asking voters what they did as they exit the polling station. You would think you couldn't go wrong with this. After all, if people can't remember who they voted for in the time it takes to walk out of the door of the hall, they probably can't remember their name or where they live.

Yet the accuracy of exit polls has been decidedly shaky down the years and in 1987 the BBC managed to produce a catastrophic one which led to viewers being told Labour had won although the Tories actually were 12 points ahead and romped home by 120 seats.

Some countries ban opinion polls during election campaigns.

Might be a good idea if Britain did the same – then the media would have to concentrate on the issues rather than treat elections like a sporting contest.

First past the post

In a horse race or athletics, the first one past the post or finishing line wins. That's obvious. It is also true for British general elections, in that the party which gets most seats is declared the winner. This is known as the first-past-the-post system and it has become increasingly discredited as voters realise that it leaves the majority of them without a genuine say in who forms the government.

At the 2005 election it took 26,906 votes on average to elect a Labour MP but 44,373 for a Tory. If that seems unfair, consider that it required a thumping 96,539 votes to elect a Liberal Democrat.

Not a single MP won the votes of more than 50 per cent of those who voted in his or her constituency. And a paltry three got the support of more than 40 per cent. Three candidates became MPs with less than 20 per cent of the votes cast, including the Respect MP George Galloway, who probably received more support when he was on *Celebrity Big Brother* pretending to be a cat lapping milk out of a saucer.

The problem is that seats are what matters, not votes. In 2005 the Conservatives actually received more votes than Labour in England yet won ninety-two fewer seats. On the other hand, in Surrey they won every seat despite getting only half the votes, so that county's residents who supported other parties are entitled to feel aggrieved.

It is even worse for minor parties. In 2005, the UK Independence Party picked up 603,298 votes and the Green Party 257,758 yet neither of them secured a single seat. Where did those seats go? Mainly to Labour, due to the unfairness of the electoral system. The party got 35 per cent of the votes nationally yet won 55 per cent of the seats – in Scotland it was 40 and 70 per cent.

There are other electoral systems. In fact, bizarrely, the UK has six different kinds of voting systems for the five different kinds of election it holds. Only for the Westminster Parliament is first-past-the-post retained. The rest have adopted a variation of proportional representation (PR), which distributes seats in some sort of correlation to the votes cast for a particular party. It is used for elections in Scotland, Wales, Northern Ireland, the European Parliament and the London Mayor. So why does the Westminster Parliament continue to dig its heels in against reform?

That's obvious. The big two, Labour and the Tories, would lose out so it's not in their interests to change. If they ever agreed to, turkeys and Christmas spring to mind.

Wise up, you voters

For years tactical voting was little more than a wild idea in the throbbing brains of political geeks but for the past few elections it has been adopted by ordinary voters to some effect.

It works like this. Say your constituency has a Conservative MP with a small majority. You would like to vote Labour but at the previous election the Labour candidate came a poor third behind the Liberal Democrat. If you back Labour anyway, not only are you throwing away your vote but the chances are that the Tory would get in again. But if you vote Lib Dem, they might manage to defeat the Conservative.

So tactical voting is a switch away from a candidate who stands no chance of winning to one who does. It doesn't give you the MP you really want but it can rid you of one you don't.

Tactical voting had particular force in the 1997 election in which Tony Blair came to power. Labour voters in unwinnable seats switched to the Liberal Democrats to throw out even more Conservative candidates than the swing would have achieved unaided.

This only makes sense under the first-past-the-post system. Obviously if you are voting under proportional representation, you can go for the candidate you want and your vote will count.

Let us pray

Christians have the Bible, Jews the Talmud and Muslims the Koran. Politicians have manifestos.

These are produced with religious fervour and published with enormous fanfare at the start of an election campaign. They set out what each party claims it will do if it wins.

The secret of writing a manifesto is to put in what your natural supporters want to hear plus, of course, a few things that will attract the floating voter, you hope, and leave out any hostages to fortune. Thus a good manifesto (from a politician's point of view) says little but gives the impression of promising much.

A bad manifesto – indeed, the worst ever produced – was Labour's in 1983 when the party was gripped by left-wing lunacy. It ran to 23,000 words, called for all sorts of extreme policies that were anathema to the vast majority of the British public and was famously described by one of their own senior figures as 'the longest suicide note in history'. It sold quite well, though. The Tories bought up thousands of copies to distribute to voters to remind them what a Labour government would mean.

Floating, not drowning

Normally someone who can't make up their mind is considered a pathetic nuisance. Not in politics. The person who flips between one party and another is known as The Floating Voter and is much pursued. The party which can attract this mythical being is the one which will win.

But are there really huge numbers of empty-headed electors who change their minds about their political allegiance as often as a teenage girl changes her dress? Actually, yes. There are certainly a lot more of them than there used to be. Political loyalty once ran deep – you were a Tory all your life or Labour until the day you died, and that was it. And that might be it for your children, as it had been for your own parents.

Nowadays voters are much more flexible, which creates more of a problem for the parties and can give unexpected results, particularly at by-elections.

So if you are canvassed during an election and don't want to be bothered again, whatever you do don't say you haven't made up your mind. That is a sure-fire way to ensure you get badgered over and over until you capitulate and say, OK, you will vote for them. Of course, if you like being the centre of attention, keep them dangling. . .

Thursday, bloody Thursday

Almost alone in the world, Britain holds elections on Thursdays. The Americans have them on Tuesdays, most of Europe on Sundays while Australia and New Zealand have chosen Saturdays.

But, rather like driving on the left, we prefer to be different. Elections don't have to be on Thursdays. By law they could be on any weekday except bank holidays or 'days of public thanksgiving or mourning'. As most voters don't get the government they want, there would be a case for saying every election is a day of mourning. And, of course, the thanksgiving of the winning party is so public it is positively vomit-inducing.

On election day, the first thing candidates and party organisers do when they wake up is look out of the window to see what the weather is like. There is an old political maxim that Labour does better when the sun shines and the Tories better when it rains. This was based on the idea that well-off Conservative voters could travel in their limousines to polling stations whatever the weather whereas cloth-capped Labour supporters, fresh in from mucking out the whippets, would refuse to venture out again because they couldn't cope with trudging through the puddles on the way to cast their votes.

Polling stations open at seven o'clock in the morning to allow people to vote on their way to work or if they are insomniacs. They close at 10 p.m. to allow people to vote on their way home from work or after they have eaten dinner – yes, dinner, not supper; another myth is that Labour voters turn out early and Tories later.

Some time before polling day every elector receives a polling card with their name and address on. Many believe they can't vote without producing theirs, rather like you have to show a bank card or a passport. This is wrong. You only have to give your name and address to the person at the polling station and they give you your ballot form. No questions asked. No proof of identity required.

Then you step into the wooden booth, pick up the Argos-like thick pencil-on-a-string inside and mark your X in the appropriate place before folding the form neatly and popping it into the black box.

End of job. Or nearly. Sitting outside the polling station will be one or more people with large rosettes, some polling cards, a pad and a biro. These have been sent along by the parties to note who has voted.

This is another tradition and, except in the tightest of marginals, is of as dubious value as looking out of the window to see if it is raining. The idea is that people who have told canvassers they will vote for Party A are 'knocked up' late on election day if they haven't been to vote yet. Even if the election in this seat is so close that every vote could make a difference, voters may have lied when they were canvassed, or they may have changed their minds, or they may have decided not to vote, or they may prefer to watch something really good on TV that evening.

So it is not likely that a particular seat will be won or lost, let alone governments fall or survive, on the brilliance of name-collecting outside polling stations. What it does do, though, is make party workers feel wanted.

Enough to give you piles

At 10 o'clock, polling stations close. The boxes containing those precious votes are loaded on to vans and driven to the hall where the count is to take place.

Of course, this isn't easy in massive rural constituencies. In a small inner-city seat, the boxes can be collected and delivered to the count in minutes. If the polling stations are spread over an area half the size of a small country, it is going to take a long time. Which is why some constituencies don't bother to start counting until the next day.

The problem about an election count, if you insist on considering it as a spectator sport, is that you get more excitement in a race to see which of two paints will dry first. It consists of people sorting out, piling up and counting pieces of paper. Thrilling eh? Well it is if you are one of the candidates or a party worker.

The people who do the actual work are mainly professionals, trained for years in banks. Little did they know when they had to go through their apprenticeship of sorting bundles of notes into fives, tens, twenties and fifties that they were merely practising for The Big One – counting ballot papers.

The forms are put in separate piles for each candidate. So if one pile is four foot high while the rest are half an inch, it's pretty clear who the winner is going to be. But they still have to count them all.

Eventually the moment comes when the returning officer gets the candidates together on a platform and reads out the results, in alphabetical order of the candidates' names. There is a certain amount of cheering.

For anyone who hasn't been through it, it is hard to understand how much emotion is involved in this procedure. It is more bowel-churning than a Cup Final with just as much euphoria for the winner (though it usually comes through more as smugness) and heartbreak for the losers.

If Sir David Attenborough ever tires of making documentaries about animals, he could turn his attention to the customs, rituals and natural history of the politician in its election-night habitat. But even the great film-maker would find it hard to explain exactly what it all means.

Winners and losers

So that's it. The great electoral process is over, the battle won and lost, the course of government set in train for the next four or five years. But remember, it isn't just about who forms the government. There are 646 Members of Parliament who have just been elected. Let's see which among them matters. Not in the sense of getting on TV a lot or being called regularly by the Speaker in the Commons, but who matters when it comes to being able to make their mark on the country and (the ultimate aim of all politicians) on history.

After the 2005 election, there were 356 Labour MPs, which left another 290 members not in the governing party. They don't matter, then, even if the leader of the opposition becomes well known and may be thought of as the next Prime Minister.

The government had ninety-six ministers from the Commons, which left 260 Labour MPs on the back benches, so they don't matter.

Of the ninety-six on the government payroll, more than fifty were whips (who keep MPs in order) or parliamentary under-secretaries, which is the lowest form of governmental life. So none of them matter.

Then there are the ministers of state, who are the seconds-in-command but rarely have any real power. Their greatest use is to be put up as the fall guy when something goes badly wrong for their boss.

Which brings it down to the Cabinet, the twenty-two senior ministers. They must surely all matter. But do they? Hardly. With devolved government, there is no real influence for the Secretaries of State for Wales, Scotland and Northern Ireland. In fact Gordon Brown thought Scottish Secretary was such a minor role he believed one could run the Ministry of Defence as well in his spare time.

Other Cabinet roles are not at the apex of power and influence either. Environment, Food and Rural Affairs? Usually considered a backwater. International Development? Not at the cutting edge. The Olympics? Yes, there is a minister in the Cabinet whose job is to organise the 2012 Olympic Games. Not part of the inner cabal, clearly.

So it comes down to the few people who really do matter: the Home Secretary, the Chancellor of the Exchequer, the Foreign Secretary, and a couple of others whose importance fluctuates depending on who they are and how matey they are with the Prime Minister.

Because, ultimately, there is only one person who really matters and that is the Prime Minister. Which is why politicians are so desperate to reach the very, very top, to stand at the peak of the political Everest and not get stuck at one of the base camps.

Anyone who thinks that isn't so should try to remember ministers from Mrs Thatcher's time or John Major's or even Tony Blair's. Exactly. The Prime Minister dwarfs them all.

It is not just a question of being the one with his or her feet under the big desk or even of personality. Today everything is expected to pass through the office of the PM and receive his personal seal of approval before being inflicted on the public.

So there you have it. Politics is a giant mound, very wide at the bottom, very narrow at the top. At the bottom are the forty-five million people who can vote, with those in marginal seats a bit higher up. Then, rising slowly up, are the tens of thousands who belong to a political party, followed by the thousands who are more involved by being councillors or organisers.

By the time you reach the few hundred who are lucky enough to become MPs, you are getting near the top. But there is still a long way to go, edging past the few dozen who make it into government and the handful who reach Cabinet office until, at the pinnacle, is the one person who matters. The Prime Minister. Having clambered up that long, steep, slippery incline, no wonder he thinks he can do what he likes to the masses down below.

Allocating scarce resources for the elderly is a major problem for politicians. Here two care-home inmates trial a new way to see who will get the pills tonight. (William West/Getty Images)

Time to take a stand

Stupid, greedy and out of touch – that's MPs

If you have got this far, your prejudices against politics in general and politicians in particular should have been confirmed. And that is without going into detail on the expenses and allowances scandal, which not only saw them ripping off taxpayers for duck houses, garlic presses, giant plasma televisions, moat-cleaning and second homes the size of mansions but left most of them baffled to understand why the public was so incensed at the revelations.

But the charge list against politicians is far bigger than that. They have created a world of their own in which almost any expense can be incurred because we, the taxpayers, pick up the bill (admittedly they pay taxes too, but when did you ever hear an MP say 'We'd better not do that, I will have to pay more tax'? Exactly. They are cocooned from the costs of real life.)

Over the years, more and more layers of bureaucrats, managers and officials have been created. These self-perpetuating strata of society are embedded in everything we do. They have been given a huge boost by the obsession with targets and league tables – some started by the Tories but most of it central to the New Labour way of doing things – which requires still more bureaucrats to collect and organise the tsunami of meaningless statistics.

They have spread like dry rot across the country. If you are in one of those jobs, it's great for you. It beats heavy lifting and is a lot less arduous than walking a police beat, trying to control a class of unruly children or struggling to cope in an accident and emergency unit. There may have been increases in the number of teachers and nurses but those are as nothing compared with the rise in pen-pushers and press officers across Whitehall.

Those people are often not employed because there is a job to do but to create a job once they are employed. Hence the endless torrent of rules and regulations that pour out and the idiotic ideas and initiatives. Volumes could be filled with examples of stupefying rubbish that keeps a lot of people in work – or, rather, is produced because people are in work and would have nothing to do if they didn't produce said rubbish. They hold meetings that last for hours and send hundreds of emails to each other. They talk in a strange language that has nothing to do with real life – about delivery, process, reaching out, stakeholders and end users. And they don't even know they're doing it.

While this is great material for comedians, columnists and right-wing commentators, it's a disaster for society. People are brainwashed into failing to think for themselves because they have come to expect someone else to think for them. Well, they must be, mustn't they, because they are being paid for doing it, the reasoning goes; although a cursory consideration of the result of this 'thinking' confirms that it is not what a sane society would describe as thought. Nevertheless, it is turning adults into children because these people who know best what's good for us are increasingly running our lives.

What has this got to do with stupid, greedy and out-of-touch MPs? Obviously, they are the ones creating this new world. A world in which the bossy class is out of control because politicians have wound them up, pointed them vaguely in that direction and then gone off to do something else mad and socially dangerous without considering the consequences of what they have already set in motion.

Can they be stopped? Yes, they can. Who is the superman (or woman) who can do it? It is you. The voter. Keep that in mind as you read on.

The explosion of bureaucracy is not the only accusation to be levelled at the way our country is being run. Incompetence is reaching new heights or plumbing new depths, depending which way you look at it. We know politicians couldn't run a bath, a whelk stall or a piss-up in a brewery not because we read it in the papers but because we have regular experience of the consequences of what they do.

Politicians and the civil servants they employ no longer waste millions of pounds of our hard-earned money, they waste billions and, with the banking bail-outs, are heading into trillion territory (a trillion being a one followed by twelve zeros). Any private company that squandered so much so often would go out of business (except the private companies hired by the government, which squander vast amounts but stay in business because the government keeps on hiring them. When Bob Dylan sang 'There's no success like failure' he was specifically referring to the British government, its employees and hirelings.)

Yes, it's disastrous and disgraceful. But there is someone who can stop it happening. You. Little old you, the voter. You and thousands like you.

Stupid, greedy and out of touch – that's voters

If we have a government and politicians who treat us as though we're idiots, that acts like an overbearing nanny, that rips us off and takes us for granted, whose fault is it? Ours, unfortunately We live in a democracy so we have the opportunity to tell them to stop it and start behaving. If this was a dictatorship and the rulers imposed their will at the point of a gun and threw opponents in jail, it would be different. Though there are always brave people in states like that who are prepared to risk their lives to fight oppression. So why is it in this cradle of democracy called the United Kingdom that we don't stand up to the nonsense of politicians?

There used to be a strong element of "'They" (with a capital T) know best'. Not only politicians but everyone in a position of authority, including doctors, teachers and bosses.

But the age of deference is dead (supposedly). We are now in a position, thanks to better education, the power of the media and bitter experience, in which we can tell our rulers not to be so bloody silly. And if they don't respond, chuck them out of office. Why don't we?

It is sadly true that a significant proportion of the British people is ignorant about politics. Not of irrelevant geeky statistics, such as what was the government majority at the 1880 general election, but of the most basic workings of the political system. Yet they are only too well aware of what is going wrong, so ignorance isn't bliss.

Then there is the greed of voters. We are too easily bribed. When given a choice between a 'tax cut' or cuts in important services, too many go for paying less tax. Then they moan when they can't get proper health treatment or education for their children or when our troops are sent off to war improperly equipped.

Anyway, tax cuts mean pennies for most of us – it's only the rich who pocket vast sums. Yet it is incredible how many people are opposed to higher taxes for people earning, say, £100,000 a year even though they only earn £25,000 themselves and will never get near a hundred grand. But they live in hope so don't want to risk being taxed more on a fantasy salary they'll never earn.

Britain today is a land in which not only is personal responsibility increasingly being taken away but millions of us are voluntarily giving up our responsibility to vote. Too many live in isolation, unaware of their neighbours or what their elected representatives are doing in their name.

If we don't say No, then the government assumes we've said Yes. We haven't and we don't like it when we discover what they have done. But we were too busy hanging on to our jobs, paying the bills, juggling family commitments and trying to remember which day is recycling day. And we are bombarded with anxiety whether it's the latest health scare, climate change or international terrorism. So it's easier to keep your head down, mind your own business and hope for the best.

The trouble is, governments have a tendency to do things that creep up on you and before you know it, they've introduced another set of rules and laws 'for our safety', which is like your granny saying 'Eat up your sprouts, they're good for you' when you know all they do for certain is make you fart.

An understandable concern about paedophiles has been used to make everyone who comes anywhere near children have to undergo criminal record checks. That didn't stop Vanessa George, a nursery worker, abusing babies in her care and it won't prevent dedicated, cunning paedophiles, but it will stop people giving music lessons, coaching sports, or helping out in schools, at cubs and brownies and on school trips.

The fear of terrorism and revulsion at terrorist attacks has changed the way we live in far more ways than interminable queues at airports.

Politicians have immense power yet they are just ordinary people, as flawed as the rest of us. We give them power if we vote for them and they get power anyway if we don't. In a way we give them more power when we don't bother to vote because we don't challenge them. It's like turning a blind eye to crime because we 'don't want to get involved' and then whingeing because criminals get away with it. We have more power than politicians because we can use our vote and make them earn it, hold them to account with it and remind them they answer to us, the voters, not the political party they belong to or some oddball idea a twenty-year-old adviser has come up with or even the editorials in the *Daily Mail*.

Yes, we have the power. And if we don't use it, we are more stupid than the politicians.

But politics has nothing to do with me

Doesn't it? If you can honestly, hand on heart, say you absolutely don't care how much tax you pay, if your kids' school isn't teaching them properly, whether you can see a doctor or get to hospital when you need to, how much your TV licence costs, how many hours and under what conditions you work, whether you can get financial help if you're unemployed or disabled, how big or small the state pension is and what care is given to old people, and if you couldn't give a damn if global warming means Norfolk could look like the landscape of *Mad Max*, then for heaven's sake stick with a useful hobby like picking fluff from your navel and wait for aliens to come and take you off.

However cynical, disillusioned and bored with politics we might be, it doesn't make sense to ignore it. Like dog mess on your shoe, ignoring politicians won't make them go away – it just means fewer people decide how our lives work. Idyllic as it may sound to hunker down, knit your own yoghurt, teach the children at home and never use public transport, doctors, police or firefighters, or buy anything including gas, electricity or water, the reality is that we have to exist alongside millions of other people and politics is the basis of how we do that.

You may not care a jot about old people's homes because you are seventeen or about schools because you haven't any children or employment rights because you don't work, but you do care about something and the chances are that one day you will be affected by most of the things politics touches. You might have children, fall sick or be out of work, and you will certainly grow old. But meanwhile what you definitely care about – in a negative way – is that you think all politicians are corrupt, only in it for themselves and don't do anything for you.

Many people sneer at those who care about the 'big' things like the environment, world peace and poverty. It's also easy to mock the little things that concern other people, like pedestrian crossings and shop opening hours, because you don't care about those irrelevancies. But much of what we take for granted has come about because of people who wanted to make the world a better place.

Politics does attract the egocentric and self-serving but at its heart it is about a desire to improve things. Make them better for individuals, better for society, better for the country and better for the world. No one goes into democratic politics wanting to make people poorer, sicker or persecuted.

On the couch with your MP

It is a question which the most brilliant of psychiatrists would struggle to answer: Why on earth would anyone want to be an MP? Or, even more baffling, why get involved in politics at all? At least an MP may have a chance of becoming a minister and has the magic initials M and P after his name, which could get him to the head of the queue for a table in a smart restaurant.

The general public thinks of politicians as lazy and self-serving, but if that were universally true, millions more people would want to join them. They'd trample you underfoot in the rush for a cushy life.

A conscientious member of Parliament actually has a ridiculously busy existence. So hectic, in fact, that you can understand why they feel wounded and unappreciated when they are accused of jumping on a gravy train.

Consider a typical week for an MP who we shall call Hectic Hector, though you might prefer Greedy Gerry. On Monday morning he wakes up in his constituency which is 200 miles from London (at least 500 MPs have constituencies more than 100 miles from Westminster). He gets a train or plane down to the capital. Then starts a remorseless procession of meetings, reading and writing letters and emails, phone calls, more meetings, dropping into the Commons chamber (especially for Prime Minister's Questions at noon on a Wednesday). Even though the Commons rises (finishes for the day, in ordinary language) at 7 p.m. on Tuesday, Wednesday and Thursday (it's 10 p.m. on Monday), there is likely to be more work after that.

On Thursday evening, or Friday morning, he will travel back to his constituency. But then, far from being able to relax with the family, comes a succession of surgeries, when he has to listen to his constituents whingeing on about their problems, plus meetings with constituency officers, when he has to listen to them whingeing on about his failings and his party's failings and the government's failings, as well as attending as many jumble sales, school fetes and garden shows as he can to show he is a caring MP playing a full part in local life. And where he meets still more constituents who whinge on about. . . you get the idea.

And remember, despite all that effort, there is a chance that these ungrateful wretches on whom he has expended so much time and attention are perfectly capable of turfing him out at the next election.

Yes, why on earth would anyone *want* to become an MP?

The question is particularly relevant at the moment. Many MPs are genuinely hurt by the public's revulsion over the expenses and allowances scandal. They believe they work long hours, incredibly hard, conscientiously and with dedication. They are convinced they perform a real service for the country and the British people.

The New Labour theme song for the 1997 election, 'Things Can Only Get Better', wasn't just a catchy tune, they meant it. Besides, there wasn't a song called 'We're Going to Be George W. Bush's Poodle and Invade Iraq'. Even the Conservative Party, which for much of its existence was more interested in conserving the way things were, as its name implies, is now hell-bent on Making Things Better.

But what about me, *me, ME?*
There are more than sixty million people in the UK and if you take away babies and young children, you still have, say, fifty million. It doesn't take a genius to realise that not every one of them has the same wishes, needs and opinions. In fact every single one of us is a bit different. So politicians have to cope with the competing demands of voters, particularly when there is a growing insistence that politics has to satisfy every foot-stamping requirement of every member of the Me Generation.

There is hardly an issue in which there are not two sides, each driven by what is best for them. Here are a few:

- Older people don't think they should have to sell the home they have lived in all their life to fund their stay in a care home. They think the state should pay. But young people struggling with a huge mortgage don't see why they should be forced to pay through their taxes for care for people who already own their homes.

- People who have got on the property ladder want to see prices keep on rocketing because it makes them richer. But those who haven't got on the first rung want lower prices so they can buy a home (after which, of course, they will want them to soar).

- Workers want all sorts of protection, including benefits such as maternity leave. Employers find the imposition of 'red tape' a real burden to keeping their businesses going.

- Farmers want good prices for their produce. Supermarkets and their customers want to keep prices low.

- Train passengers want money spent on improving services. People who never use the railways and always drive demand that public money is spent on roads instead.

And so it goes on. For each of us has a unique set of circumstances so each of us has our own demands on the state. The problem for politicians is that they have to reconcile the irreconcilable, to square a circle of infinite circumference.

It can't be done, of course, so they head for compromise, while trying to make as many constituents as possible think they are getting what they asked for (how daft – we really aren't that stupid. Are we?).

The other impossible issue they have to deal with is tax. All these services have to be paid for. The pensions, the health service, the armed forces, education and the rest.

Even though politicians regularly insist they are going to bring down taxes, no one suggests they should be abolished. They have existed as long as human society. It doesn't mean anyone enjoys paying them – have you ever met someone who said 'Hey, I really, *really* enjoy paying my tax. I *so* look forward to whipping out the cheque book and handing over wodges of my income. I always round the sum up – that makes me feel warm inside'?

No, just about everyone complains about the tax they pay, whether they are very rich and hand over huge sums or low paid and have to give a disproportionate part of their income to the taxman. Most of us can't understand why someone receiving a million pound bonus objects to paying half of it in tax. After all, they still have half a million, which is more than most of us earn in a lifetime. Yet the lucky few who receive those massive bonuses don't see why they should hand over still more money when they are already giving tens of thousands of pounds every year to the taxman and not getting much back in return.

It is true that some state spending is a waste – a great deal of it, according to organisations such as the TaxPayers' Alliance, a fundamentalist group that never accepts any taxpayers' money is spent well, let alone wisely.

Such fanatics should tell us which of these activities should be stopped so that less tax needs to be raised:

- Transport – from building and maintaining roads to high-speed rail links, bus services and pensioners' passes.
- Education – providing free and adequate education for everyone between five and sixteen as well as nurseries, universities and colleges, evening classes and apprenticeships. All need buildings and equipment as well as people to run them from teachers to dinner ladies.
- Health – from A&E and the ambulance service to cancer

drugs, keyhole surgery, having a baby, mental health provision, dentistry or simply getting a hearing aid or glasses.

- Social services – there but for the grace of. . . go all of us who could one day need help with housing, home care, disability, domestic abuse, family breakdown, a place of safety, money if we couldn't earn it ourselves and a thousand and one other things.

- Crime – the police, prisons, courts, probation service and the legal system.

Appreciating what our taxes go on is an important element in understanding how politics works but politicians are loath to explain it. If they would actually come out and say, for instance, that £74,863,241.26 (to pluck a number at random) is spent on nurses or pensions for the over-eighties or repairing motorways, we would see exactly where the money is going. As it is, the public is increasingly convinced that their hard-earned cash is ripped savagely from purses and wallets to be frittered away on yoga lessons for one-eyed Bulgarian lesbians or dress-making seminars for under-seven asylum seekers or flesh-eating plants for the foyer at the Agriculture Department or to go straight into the pockets of those greedy, grasping Members of Parliament. Instead of appreciating that most of our taxes go to make life better for the old, young, unemployed or other needy sections of the population.

The hardest word
It has five letters and two syllables, should trip off the tongue but is rarely heard on the lips of British politicians. Sorry. There, it's not that difficult, is it? Yet they find it almost impossible to say, some more than others (G. Brown, for one – pathologically incapable of getting the word out).

We all make mistakes, some of us more than others. Some people make big mistakes and pay for it with their jobs, marriages or even their lives. Politicians are seen by the punters as making mistake after mistake, some of them enormous with startling consequences, yet still they refuse to acknowledge that they got it wrong, let alone actually apologise.

Not only does that lead to voters treating them with contempt because these alleged grown-ups won't do what every well-brought-up five-year-old is taught to do and say sorry for the political equivalent of knocking over the milk jug or being rude to Granny, it makes them question why they should have anything to do with them.

When highly paid public servants make mistakes that cost lives, whether in Afghanistan, Iraq, Haringey or Bristol, we're appalled and rightly so. Even more when they apparently get away with it, the ultimate insult being when they won't say sorry, just 'We'll learn from our mistakes', though that is when they actually admit mistakes were made.

While the big mistakes are the ones which hit the headlines, it is the gradual drip-drip of stupidity and incompetence that we all experience which most undermines belief in politicians.

It's the printing of leaflets telling police officers how to ride a bike, the over-zealous health and safety jobsworths who stop children playing outdoors while another government department commissions a report on why children don't play outdoors. It's the nonsense of scrapping cookery lessons in schools and wondering why there's an obesity epidemic. It's launching expensive national schemes to encourage volunteering and community spirit at the same time as treating every adult as a potential paedophile and making ridiculous rules that mean people can't use village halls and community centres. It's setting targets that mean if an ambulance crew gets to an emergency within ten minutes that's good even if the person they're going to has been dead for days, but if they take eleven minutes to get somewhere but save a life that doesn't count. Or shunting patients from where they could get treatment to where they won't because no one is allowed to be on a trolley for more than four hours.

Let's hear it for the dead guys

Here is an interesting thing about our attitude to politicians. On the whole we hate them, think they are mercenary, incompetent and haven't a clue what they are doing. But there are a few who are admired, even eulogised.

These divide into two categories. The living, who are all from other countries (take a bow Nelson Mandela), and the dead.

Nothing does more for a politician's reputation than death. However poorly he was thought of in life, however he was traduced, insulted and considered to be venal and incompetent, once he has passed on he may be suddenly revered.

The best example of the lack of appreciation of British voters is their attitude towards Winston Churchill. Here was the man reckoned to be the greatest Prime Minister of the twentieth century, indeed, one of the greatest ever, who inspired the nation to victory in the Second World War. And when the war was over, the voters threw him out. What ingratitude.

Clement Attlee, who beat Churchill in the 1945 election, was himself ditched despite introducing the National Health Service, generally considered to be British government's greatest peacetime achievement of the twentieth century.

Margaret Thatcher still has her swivel-eyed fan club but she is more condemned than admired by the population as a whole. In time, posterity may well elevate her to the level of adulation currently adopted by her most devoted adherents.

Older voters shake their heads and mutter that politics today has not produced a Churchill, Attlee or Thatcher. But when they were in power, people were bemoaning the lack of great leaders. Churchill was a virtual outcast until thrust into power by the wartime crisis while Mrs Thatcher was mocked in her early years and hated in her later ones.

That is not to say it isn't hard to see how any of today's politicians will ever rise above mediocrity. But that may be our failing, not theirs.

The point is, they have to be given a chance. Only today's politicians can tackle today's problems. If they don't do it, we are in a real mess.

On with the rose-tinted spectacles

With so many things wrong with the country today – and more than a few have been set out in this book – it's comforting to look back to a bygone age and imagine that things were so much better then. Frankly, it's not true. While some things may be worse, many are better and that is entirely due to politics.

For the most obvious changes, look outside Britain. It's almost impossible to believe that America, land of the free, was still segregating blacks and whites in the 1960s. There wouldn't be a President Obama, widely hailed as one of the good guys of politics, if politicians hadn't got involved in the fight for equality and civil rights. Nor would Nelson Mandela have got out of Robben Island jail if it hadn't been for years of campaigning against apartheid and the pressure applied by politicians who boycotted South Africa's hateful white regime.

Go further back and you begin to see the great social changes made in this country. The abolition of slavery. The ending of child labour. The creation of a welfare state instead of the brutality of the poorhouse, which separated husbands and wives. The provision of education for every child until the age of sixteen. The scrapping of the medieval law which banned a married woman from owning property. Not just the ending of capital punishment but stopping it being applied to children who stole food because they were starving.

Parliament outlawed women and children working in mines, introduced old-age pensions and unemployment benefit, cleared shameful areas of slums and provided millions of homes – though most have subsequently been sold off. They cleared up the air which used to be thick with smog given off by coal and killed countless people every winter. They brought peace to Northern Ireland (though they did much to create civil war before), they gave Scotland its first parliament for 300 years and Wales its own assembly, they outlawed sexual and racial discrimination, they allowed shopping on Sundays and pubs to open when we want a drink.

They joined the Common Market, membership of which (as the European Union) has brought peace and increased prosperity to our continent, despite what the anti-Europeans say. They introduced child benefit and family allowances and tax credits to help struggling parents. And a raft of benefits to help struggling pensioners. They gave workers paid holidays, maternity and paternity leave, health and safety protection and a minimum wage.

Then there are the social changes which make this a fairer, decent, less harsh society, like allowing divorce and legalising homosexual relationships.

Over a number of years, they also increased the franchise so not only property-owning men could vote. They gave it to women, too, after a struggle. And they lowered the voting age to eighteen because if you can fight and die for your country at that age, you ought to be allowed to vote for the people who send you to war.

The moment of truth

So finally it comes down to this. On one side there is the distorted, ridiculous, unrepresentative political system populated by self-serving egotists. On the other are the remarkable achievements they and their predecessors have made to the things which make this country what it is. OK, admittedly for bad as well as good. But let's agree that the good outweighs the bad.

When we think about politics, the image is all to do with what goes on at Westminster, of the Prime Minister and opposition leader shouting at each other across the despatch box, of distortions and lies told, and, recently, of the greed of the expenses and allowances scandal.

But politics is just as much about you and the other 45,999,999 registered voters. There are plenty of good reasons why you shouldn't vote or why you could throw your vote away on a silly party or, worse, an unworthy one. None of them are good enough, though.

There is twisted logic in the idea that people who think politicians aren't up to doing the job don't go out to vote and so leave in place precisely those people they think aren't up to it. How daft is that?

Don't get mad, get even

You can get as angry as you like but it won't change anything. Letting off steam may feel good but if what you really want is to achieve something, to get back at the bad politicians, you need to be constructive.

The simplest and most effortless way is simply to use your vote. If you want to go further, get involved. Go to meetings, write letters, make a nuisance of yourself. Maybe even join a political party. Become a school governor or sign up for other local organisations.

You could even become a councillor. Or really stick your neck out and get involved with – or lead – campaigns.

In a democratic society, all these avenues are open to you. So is not voting, hunkering down in the bunker and pulling the blankets over your head. But that's not an avenue: it's a dead end.

Here is a brief plan on how *you* can take action.

Vote or veto?

It is a common delusion among the non-voting classes that politicians care if they don't vote. Afraid that isn't so. They certainly get exercised about the drop-off in turnout at elections, and a look of intense concern may come over their faces when you inform them that you will not be partaking in the democratic process at the next election, but what will most upset them is if you say you are going to support their opponent.

Not voting doesn't stop anything. It isn't a veto, although if all the non-voters got together and marked an X for 'None of them', that would send a shockwave through the system. But that isn't going to happen, so failing to vote allows you to be dismissed as a member of the Apathy Party rather than recognising you as a paid-up supporter of the I Hate Them All Party.

Voting is easy. All you have to do is get your name on the electoral register, wander down to the polling station on election day and mark an X on your ballot paper. It helps if you have decided who to vote for, of course. If you think you might be away on election day or are worried that the old war wound could be playing up and you won't be able to stagger along to the school hall down the road, you can register for a postal vote.

Remember, there is no right or wrong way to cast your vote. In this country you don't get victimised, banged up in prison or murdered if you don't support the victorious party, even if some politicians give the impression that's what they would like to do to dissidents.

It is your choice, it's secret and you can give your X to whoever you like on the list.

You may think your single little vote won't affect anything. But if everyone who thought like that used their vote, just imagine what a difference it could make.

Action stations!

If you have been persuaded to go this far in the democratic process, how about taking the next step? You might need a lie-down after the exertion of voting, but when you have fully recovered, why not get involved in something else? Like going to meetings. Like confronting your MP wherever you can track him or her down and asking questions. And more questions. And still more questions. And insisting on getting answers. Answers that mean something. Answers which reply to the questions you asked, not to some tangential subject like the shortage of cod in the North Sea (unless you are a fisherman and that is the question you asked).

Challenge authority. Laugh at the nonsense. Expose the incompetence and stupidity.

You may consider that this would be a waste of time. Why should you succeed where John Humphrys, Jeremy Paxman and Richard and Judy have struggled? But you may be surprised at the reaction you get when a politician is not trapped in the media headlights. Many of them actually like to interact with the public.

You don't have to ask about huge national or international issues, or get involved in those. Try something that matters to where you live. Like a hospital that's underperforming. Or a post office threatened with closure. Or plans slipped in by dodgy property developers. Or the state of public transport or the roads.

These don't get the same national publicity as going to war or an economic collapse but they sure as hell matter to your neighbours.

Send letters to the local paper. Leave comments on the MP's website – after all, they say they want to hear what constituents think. Be a nuisance. Stand up for your rights.

The last word

One of the most annoying things about politicians is that they always want to have the last word. The classic example is the Prime Minister's answer to the leader of the opposition's sixth and final question at PMQs each week. It is the equivalent of a seven-year-old sticking out his tongue and saying 'Yah boo, you smell and your sister smells, so there!' Absolutely pathetic.

But you can stop politicians having the last word by having it yourself. You and every other voter.

The last word is the message you leave in the ballot box on election day.

And the first and last word in democracy is: Vote.

About the authors

David Seymour's journalistic career began on the *John O'Groat Journal*. He spent most of his working life on Fleet Street on the *Daily Mirror, Today* and the *Daily Mail*. He was political editor of the Mirror Group for more than a decade and later worked (briefly) as leader writer on the *Daily Mail*. He was the *Mirror*'s readers' editor and founded *Student Mirror*, as well as being a regular broadcaster.

Since leaving Fleet Street he has combined journalism with consultancy, and wrote *Reporting Poverty*, a guide for journalists. He is a board member of the Countryside Alliance and a trustee of Headliners, which helps disadvantaged young people through journalism.

Jo Phillips is an award-winning journalist and former spin doctor. Her career has spanned politics, public affairs and media. She has worked for all the UK's major broadcasters, was editor of the Radio 5 Live politics show *Sunday Service*, produced live TV coverage of party conferences and has played a key role in local, European and general elections.

She was director of communications for Bob Geldof's media company, Ten Alps and was heavily involved in Live8.

Jo was Paddy Ashdown's press secretary, and she has worked on the Home Office's Y Vote campaign, been a non-executive director of a local health authority and a prison visitor, driven in rallies across Syria, stood for Parliament and chaired a crime prevention panel. She is a West Ham United season ticket holder.